RESET

▸YOUR LIFE

RESET

▶ YOUR LIFE

MAKE A NEW START

JOSEPH W.
WALKER III

W PUBLISHING GROUP

AN IMPRINT OF THOMAS NELSON

Published in Nashville, Tennessee, by W Publishing Group, an imprint of Thomas Nelson.

Thomas Nelson titles may be purchased in bulk for educational, business, fund-raising, or sales promotional use. For information, please e-mail SpecialMarkets@ThomasNelson.com.

Library of Congress Control Number: 2015910542

ISBN 978-0-7180-4175-5

Printed in the United States of America

15 16 17 18 19 RRD 6 5 4 3 2 1

CONTENTS

CHAPTER 1

GETTING THE MOST FROM THIS BOOK

Any book worth reading is a dialogue. It is a place where author and reader meet, where words on a page or screen invite reaction—thought, contemplation, imagination, emotion, and, ultimately, action. What's more, if a book has a spiritual aim, as this one does, there is a third party in the conversation. God is part of the equation, for where two or more meet in his name, he is there (Matt. 18:20).

This book is an outgrowth of my ministry and that of my church. It aims to engage you in the process and possibilities of being reset. I hope you will allow the three-way conversation about to take place between you, me, and the Spirit of God to serve as the doorway to rejuvenation and renewal. Let this be your opportunity to go back to that place where, as a new Christian, you were on fire for the things of the Lord, where prayer and love and service excited every cell in your body. I see such renewals happen every Sunday in my churches in Nashville, and I want to extend that possibility to everyone who reads this book.

To get the most from this book, ask the Holy Spirit to be part of the process. Wherever you are reading this—in your quiet place at home, on your lunch break from work, in an airplane, or on the beach:

- Pause for a moment and prepare yourself mentally to engage with what you are about to read.
- Put yourself in the stories as you read them, looking for phrases and situations that speak to you.
- React! Let the stories and text excite you, let them make you think, let them press your buttons!
- Then ask yourself, "Why is this story having such an effect on me?"
- Finally, and most importantly, ask, "How can I apply this in my life?"

Ask the Holy Spirit to be part of the process.

Our dialogue will be facilitated by discussion points at the end of every chapter designed to get you thinking and to allow you to draw on your knowledge, experience, failures and successes, disappointments, and dreams, for it is only when you're fully engaged that this three-way conversation can carry you forward.

Where are we headed? We are aiming for reset. We're looking for that place where you slough off your old skin and walk, fresh and invigorated, into the joys and challenges ahead.

I hope all of that sounds inspirational, but I hope even more that it sounds eminently practical because that's what I have in mind. This is not a theological text. It's not an academic treatise. This is a book about the Christian life and how to live it successfully, drawing lessons from the people whose stories inhabit the Bible. These were people who sometimes found that the new had worn off. They sometimes lost their edge. They resisted their calling. They were willing to settle. In other words, they were men and women just like you and me. At some point, though, they heard the Spirit of God calling them to renew. When they said yes, they were changed, just as you can be.

That doesn't mean it was instantly easy for them, or that it will be easy for you. But you will see, time after time, how heeding the call to renew can make you into someone capable of miracles, someone for whom the extraordinary, the awe-inspiring, can be not just possible but a way of life.

So how can you approach this book on a practical level? What can you hope to gain from it that will change your life and how you live it? Let's start with what you're facing right now. What are the stumbling blocks in your life? What are the questions you find difficult to answer? Here are some of the questions people commonly face as they grapple with life:

- Did I choose the right major?
- Should I stay in this job?
- Is it too late to change careers?
- Why is it so hard to find and keep a good relationship?
- Why is this marriage so difficult?
- I feel like I'm always pouring myself into other people and their problems. When will it be my time?
- What could I do with my leisure time that would make me feel useful to my neighborhood, my city, the world?
- Why do I feel so stale spiritually?
- Why don't I take more responsibility for my own health and well-being?
- What is my purpose here on earth?

Once you know what the questions are, you can start looking for answers.

Once you know what the questions are, you can start looking for answers. Remember, *we can't fix what we won't face.* Once you can put a name on it, you can start to apply the principles in this book to it, and once you do that, you can start walking with God toward a better life.

So as you read, underline. Highlight. Take notes. Write in the margins. Read this book with a friend, your spouse, your book club, or a small group at church. Look for ways to bring the principles here alive in your own life.

And prepare to reset.

How to Read the Bible for Reset

We don't have to fly blind when it comes to the process of being reset. We don't need to reinvent the wheel. Countless men and women have been on the path before us. This book draws on the experience and wisdom of so many people I have known through the years—those who did it right and those who did it wrong—as well as many people who were reset in the pages of Scripture. I have taken their lessons and tried to present them in a way that gives you a clear picture of the path to reset, the process of reset, and the results of reset.

As we prepare, there are specifics I can share that may help light your way. Allow me to distill some of the mindsets and techniques that you might find helpful.

Let's start with Scripture. Reading the Bible is an art and a science. It is where we interact with the living God. The Word is such that each of us can glean from it the lessons and principles we need. God sometimes states rules, but the Bible consists largely of stories, because God knows that is how we as human beings learn best. We will be visiting a number of people in the Old and New Testaments, interacting with them and with their stories as presented by writers indwelt with God's Holy Spirit.

For instance, we will be reading about Saul, whose reset turned a violent enemy of the Way, as early Christianity was called in his day, into the man who would write most of the letters found in the New Testament, teaching us how to walk the path Jesus laid out for us.

Throughout this book you will find citations for verses written by Paul that relate his story. These passages may consist of just two or three verses. It is often helpful to read more, to see these verses in context by reading the entire chapter from the Bible before you proceed.

In preparing to read Scripture, be ready to concentrate. Reread as necessary. Try to picture the action and hear the dialogue. These are not just words. They are depictions of events important enough to be included in the Bible. God wants us to be familiar with them. Then once you've read a section with your full attention, relax for a moment and let the scene permeate you. Let it seep into your heart as well as your mind.

Now let's look at what God is saying—to you. Let's look at Acts 9, where Saul encounters the Lord on the road to Damascus:

> Then Saul, still breathing threats and murder against the disciples of the Lord, went to the high priest and asked letters from him to the synagogues of Damascus, so that if he found any who were of the Way, whether men or women, he might bring them bound to Jerusalem. (vv. 1–2)

As you read it over, make sure you understand the situation. Try to picture the conversation and the room in which it takes place, letting the scene play in your head. Then, when you have taken it into your head and heart, turn inward. How are you like Saul? Most of us can vouch that we've not breathed murderous threats against Christians, although some of us come from backgrounds violent enough that we can identify.

Look honestly at your life. If your disagreements with or dislike of people have been strong enough to lead to threats or actual violence, look at whether those days are truly behind you. If they are, thank God for your deliverance from them and vow to stay on the path of good relations with others. If you are still involved in that kind of destructive behavior, pray for the willingness and ability to overcome and be free of your darker nature—pray for reset.

And if you honestly say those kinds of threats and violence are no longer part of you, look for how this scripture might apply anyway. No Bible verse stands completely alone. We read it in the context of the entire Bible. Remember that Jesus said,

> "You have heard that it was said to those of old, 'You shall not murder, and whoever murders will be in danger of the judgment.' But I say to you that whoever is angry with his brother without a cause shall be in danger of the judgment." (Matt. 5:21–22)

We are called to a higher standard. We are not expected simply not to kill, not to steal, not to commit adultery. Jesus made clear that we are not to remain angry, not to covet another's possessions, not to lust in our hearts. So these

7

We are called to a higher standard. verses apply to us if we harbor grudges, if we judge others harshly, if we look down on those around us. If we truly want to follow Christ, we are as liable for reset when it comes to anger as we are when it comes to murder, for lust as much as for adultery. We let the verses speak to us and convict us, and we pray for the strength to move forward.

Let's look at one more verse from Acts chapter 9:

> As he journeyed he came near Damascus, and suddenly a light shone around him from heaven. Then he fell to the ground, and heard a voice saying to him, "Saul, Saul, why are you persecuting Me?" (vv. 3–4)

Again, most of us don't get knocked to the ground by lights and voices, but once we've pictured the scene, the question becomes, "How does the Lord speak to me?" For most of us, we hear that still, small voice, often drowned out yet there and unmistakable. It's the tug of our conscience. Often it's supplemented by Bible verses that speak to us, by things people say that ring true with us or convict us, by sermons, by song lyrics. So ask yourself, "What is the voice of God calling me to do?" The answer is personal to each individual, but each of us is indwelt with the voice of God, calling us to God's will. And each of us is given the ability to respond to that call.

How to Pray for Reset

Now, about prayer. Remember, our goal is to seek God's will and align with it, before, during, and after reset.

Before reset—we hear the call. It may be faint, but our spirits are finely tuned to God's Spirit. It is the world that drowns out that voice. Even if we are not there yet, if sin still has us, if our vices still control us, we can recognize the voice. Once we know that we are being called to change, to reset, we have the opportunity to ask God to lead us. Prayer can be simple: "Oh, God, lead me to reset. Let your call awaken me. Let your voice reach my ears and my spirit. Let your presence continue to grow inside me."

During reset—we see the process of resetting involves every aspect of our lives. Our prayer as we are being reset might be, "Lord, reset my mind, my heart, my spirit. Let every aspect of me awaken to a new awareness of you and your mission for me."

After reset—we look for the strength to carry out our mission. "Lord, I feel your power flowing through me. Please help me to stay focused on doing what I know you would have me to do."

This book will walk you through everything you need to know about the process of being reset in God. It will offer background, examples, and practical tips designed to get you back in the game of life. As you read this book, I pray you are inspired, challenged, and empowered to reset your life. The world is waiting on you.

REFLECTIONS

- Make your own list of the questions life has raised within your spirit. Be sure to include the things that are troubling you.
- Write your own prayer, one that asks God to prepare you for the task of being reset.

CHAPTER 2

RESET: THE CHOICE IS NOW

The modern smartphone is a wondrous device. It would take pages to list all the things it can do, but a small list should paint the picture: it's a camera, stopwatch, photo album, video screen, song library, GPS-enabled navigator, texting device, compass, weather report, alarm clock, address book, search engine, and voice-activated personal assistant. It'll even let you make phone calls!

Need it to do more? It's also a store, with access to software that lets you do anything from identify the constellations to sell your home. They aren't kidding when they say, "There's an app for that."

It's pretty impressive and, like it or not, we depend on it. So you can imagine what it felt like when my smartphone went bad. Oh, it still worked, sort of, but the reception was spotty, and it would drop calls and sometimes lock up on me altogether. I'd have to turn it off and restart it to get it working again.

I'm not a techie—I don't know a thing about malware or spybots or viruses. I just know my smartphone was no longer as smart as I needed it to be. So I went back to where I'd bought it and talked to someone who *was* a techie. I told him what was happening and he took a look at the phone.

"You're going to need a reset," he said.

"But I've reset it," I said.

"No," he said, "you've rebooted it. That may help with your immediate lockup, but it doesn't do a thing to deal with the built-up problems your phone has accumulated."

"So what are we talking about?'

"A hard reset," he said. "It's also called a factory reset. It strips the phone of all the applications and settings you've added and everything that's been slipped into it by hackers and restores it to the state it was in when it left the factory."

I was still back on the "strips the phone" part. "You mean I'm going to lose all my data?" I said.

"Just what isn't backed up," he said. "But let me ask you, are you willing to go through life with a phone that's this unpredictable, that's running this badly?"

"No," I said.

"Well, are you willing to lose a few things to get it back?"

"I guess I am," I said. I thought it through for a minute and then said, "On second thought, I'm absolutely willing to do what it takes."

RESET: THE CHOICE IS NOW

"Then let's do the reset. And I can guarantee you'll like having a phone that feels brand-new again."

He was right. I walked out of there with a phone I could get excited about.

You Are Created for Wonderful Things

You are so much more valuable than any smartphone or computer. As marvelous as they are, both pale in comparison with the riches inside your mind and heart. You were created by God for wonderful things. You are capable of love and friendship, of productivity and creativity. You can launch a career, start a family, improve the community, make this a better world. And, ultimately, you have been chosen to participate in eternal life with its Author.

But all of us get stale. All of us at one time or another find ourselves operating at less-than-peak capacity. Your mind is crammed with a lifetime of input—information and experiences—and it is important that it be not just updated but reset periodically. Romans 12:2 says, "And do not be conformed to this world, but be transformed by the renewing of your mind, that you may prove what is that good and acceptable and perfect will of God."

Unbeknownst to you, some of the information in your mind and heart has been corrupted. You've misremembered and misrepresented, you've mislabeled and mistranslated, you've misapplied and mismanaged. You've taken shortcuts

Your mind is crammed with a lifetime of input—information and experiences—and it is important that it be not just updated but reset periodically.

and cut corners. You've assigned blame and held grudges. You've done things you shouldn't have and avoided things you should have done. Like the rest of us, you have not only allowed but often welcomed the imperfections that have made operating at full capacity all but impossible.

Nothing but a hard reset will realign and recalibrate your data so that you once again possess the ability to determine the good, acceptable, and perfect will of God. Without a reset, your judgment will remain cloudy, and you'll find it difficult to distinguish between good and bad, acceptable and unacceptable, perfect and imperfect.

There are levels of imperfection, degrees of disconnectedness from God. Maybe you're just not as productive as you should be. Or maybe your life is in complete disarray.

So many people go through this life seemingly empty, devoid of passion and purpose. It's not that those things don't exist within them. It's just that sometimes they need to be reignited. So many men and women feel that they're simply bystanders, sitting on the sidelines, passively watching the action on the court. Maybe you've fouled out, maybe you've been injured. Perhaps you've taken too many elbows or maybe you've just given up.

Moving from that place to where you can begin to fulfill

your God-given assignments is going to require a reset. In fact, you may already feel the Spirit tugging at you, telling you that's exactly what you need.

Making It Personal

Look inside. The process of reset begins with feeling that tug, hearing that call. So, ask yourself: Do you need to reset your marriage? Your career? Your finances? Your friendships? Do you need to reset your focus? Where else in your life might you need to reset—to shake off the mistakes of the past and get back in the game?

It is not God's will for you to be on the sidelines, bruised and battered. Yes, you may have been through tough times. You may have had more than your share of pain and heartache. But it's how you react to such situations that is key. Remaining a victim, wallowing in self-pity, succumbing to apathy—these are not solutions. They lead nowhere.

I don't want to minimize what you've been through, but there is a time for crying and a time for action. Tears and sweat are a lot alike. Both are comprised of water and salt. But while tears will earn you sympathy, sweat will earn you success. When you reset your way of thinking about life, you will see results. Getting reset will get the bugs and viruses out of your relationships,

It is not God's will for you to be on the sidelines, bruised and battered.

your job, and your finances. It can rejuvenate every aspect of your being.

Reset is not easy, but it is often necessary, and the key, once we recognize the need, is willingness. So ask yourself, *Am I willing to lose things I might regard as precious in order to gain even more?*

Life is about choices. Each of us will face that moment when the choice is to reset or stay where we are, and the decisions we make now will affect the rest of our lives. We reviewed some of the situations that give us trouble in the first chapter—school, job, relationships—and the question now becomes, *Do I have the courage to step out from the shadows of those situations and into the light of reset?*

But what about that great fear that a hard reset will cause you to lose data—in the form of people, places, and things you cling to? That's why there are backups. If you reset to align more fully with God, he will have your back. Rest assured that all essential knowledge is backed up in storage with God. Everything you need will be accessible. The information that is truly lost needed to be erased from your hard drive to allow you to run more efficiently and rapidly. That is the point of a reset. Most likely, the lost data contributed to your data corruption and to the overload that led to your need for a reset in the first place.

Am I willing to lose things I might regard as precious in order to gain even more?

I could have chosen to live with a subpar phone. After all, I would have still had a phone. I simply would have had to accept that its capacity was greatly diminished, that I would not be able to utilize all the functions it was capable of performing. And to this day it still would be dropping important calls.

What about you? Are you content to operate at less than capacity? Or are you willing to reset? Let's look at two examples set for us in the Old Testament—Esther, who answered the call to reset in the face of pressure that would have dissuaded many of us, and Hosea, who exemplifies God's love even for those of us for whom reset is a halting process, and who demonstrates the riches available for us in relationship with him.

Esther's Choice: For Such a Time as This

"Yet who knows whether you have come to the kingdom
for such a time as this?"
—ESTHER 4:14

The choice to reset is yours. No one can make it for you. But the consequences are never solitary. They affect not only you as an individual but also all those who are connected to you. In few places is this clearer than in the book of Esther.

Esther was an orphan raised by her cousin, Mordecai. They were the descendants of Jews carried away by Nebuchadnezzar, king of Babylon, generations earlier. They lived in Shushan, the capital city of the Persian Empire, which stretched from India to Ethiopia. The king was looking for a

The choice to reset is yours. No one can make it for you. But the consequences are never solitary.

new queen, and beautiful young women were brought to the palace from throughout the kingdom. Among them was Esther, whom the Bible describes as "lovely and beautiful." Each of these young women was prepared for a year, and Esther was the favorite of the man readying them for presentation to the king.

Throughout, Esther concealed her Jewish background, as Mordecai had instructed her. Meanwhile, Mordecai paced and fretted in front of the court. He need not have worried. The king, says Esther 2:17, "loved Esther more than all the other women, and she obtained grace and favor in his sight more than all the virgins." He made her his queen and "made a great feast, the Feast of Esther" (v. 18).

Meanwhile, Mordecai learned about a plot by two door-keepers to kill the king, and he told Esther, who "informed the king in Mordecai's name" (v. 22). The plot was confirmed, and both men were hanged.

Not long afterward, Mordecai refused to bow down and pay homage to a prince whom the king had promoted above all others. Haman, the prince, was furious. He told the king that because the Jews had their own laws "and they do not keep the king's laws" (3:8), they should be destroyed. The king agreed, decreeing that every Jew in the kingdom be killed and all their possessions taken.

Mordecai was inconsolable, and when Esther reached out to him, he asked that she intercede with the king. Esther told him that no one, not even the queen, went before the king without being summoned, at the risk of death. But Mordecai said,

> "Do not think in your heart that you will escape in the king's palace any more than all the other Jews. For if you remain completely silent at this time, relief and deliverance will arise for the Jews from another place, but you and your father's house will perish. Yet who knows whether you have come to the kingdom for such a time as this?" (4:13–14)

Think of all that had just been dropped in Esther's lap! She was a young Jewish woman thrown into a courtly world, trained to think, speak, and act like the queen of a great empire. And yet she had hidden her true nature from all of those in the court, the way many hide their Christianity when they are with people they think might make fun of it or treat its adherents as somehow lesser. Now she faced a huge decision. She had position, ease, and comfort. Remaining silent would ensure her safety. And yet the plea of the cousin who had raised her, the cries of her people, and the voice of God all stirred within her. Listening to that stirring and speaking out could well cost Esther not just her position but her life. Such might be the price of the reset she was being called toward.

In that moment she weighed not just the potential price but the potential gain. She knew too that she had to prepare herself, and she enlisted the aid of the entire community whose fate she might well hold in her hand. "Go," she said, in a message sent to Mordecai, "gather all the Jews who are present in Shushan, and fast for me; neither eat nor drink for three days, night or day. My maids and I will fast likewise. And so I will go to the king, which is against the law; and if I perish, I perish!" (4:16).

We must be prepared for reset, and Esther is a great example of the lengths sometimes necessary to be fully ready. Few people take preparation as seriously as she did, and the reason is clear—she knew the consequences she faced going in.

There is so much more to learn from Esther's example. She knew enough to tap in to the strength of her community and her God. Few things can ensure successful reset as working in partnership with those who have gone before. By the simple act of telling a friend, pastor, or Christian colleague that your aim is to renew your spirit, your commitment will assure that there is additional strength, wisdom, and experience to draw from.

Esther's diligence helped prepare her mentally and spiritually for her task, and when she made herself visible to the king, "she found favor in his sight" (5:2). He offered her whatever she wished, up to half the kingdom.

It's important to note that Esther didn't simply make her plea. She knew the king's character, what might sway him and what would not, and she knew better than to rush. She asked that the king invite the prince to a banquet she

> We must be prepared for reset, and Esther is a great example of the lengths sometimes necessary to be fully ready.

prepared. At that banquet, she requested that both attend a second banquet the following night. The delay was part of God's timing. The prince, who was sure that he would benefit from Esther's pending request, saw Mordecai standing in the king's gate, and he was filled with hatred for him. With his family, he decided to prepare gallows to hang him.

During the night, while the king was unable to sleep, he was reminded of Mordecai's great service to him, and he asked what honor had been shown to him. When he learned that no honor had been shown to Mordecai, the king asked Haman, "What shall be done for the man whom the king delights to honor?" (6:6).

Haman, filled with hubris, believed he was the honoree, and he described lavish honors he fully expected to be bestowed upon himself. When the king instead told him to provide those honors to Mordecai, Haman was doubly distraught. Then, at the banquet, Esther exposed the fact that she was among those to be killed in Haman's plot, and the king had Haman hanged on the very gallows meant for Mordecai. The queen received his house and appointed Mordecai to oversee it. It was then that she implored the king to spare all of her people from Haman's plot, and he granted her request and gave the Jews the power to defend and avenge themselves.

To this day, Esther's example is still alive. Her reset and the saving of the kingdom's Jews are commemorated in the holiday of Purim. But is it alive in your own heart?

What about the example you set? You may not get to

affect the lives of so many people, but you are no less important in your own way. If you are in need of reset and decline
it, what about the younger brother or sister who sees that
you have drifted from the Christian life you once embraced
so strongly? What about those in the neighborhood who
see one more promising young person heading in the wrong
direction? What about the friends and family members who
look to you as an example?

Your reset can change the lives of all the people who
see your rededication, who benefit from the good that ema-
nates from a life that has been rekindled
and repurposed.

Your reset can change the lives of all the people who see your rededication.

No one can make the decision to reset
for you, but countless people can benefit if
reset is what you choose. That is the power
of relationship, and Hosea is a textbook
case in the art of relationship with God.

Hosea: The Choice to Love

Ours is no cold, distant deity. Ours is not the God of the
Deists, who set the universe in motion like a watchmaker
but has no day-to-day involvement with it. Since the very
beginning of time, God's desire has been to be in relationship with his creation. God did everything he could to make
certain that man knew just how much he loved him. Even

though man quickly disappointed God through disobedience, God has been steadfastly proving that he loves us—in spite of ourselves. We have the ever-present choice to enter into, sustain, and renew a relationship with him.

In experiencing God's love, we come to realize something very important. Love is never defined by the one who is loved. It is defined by the lover. The one loved does not possess the capacity to understand the depth of the lover's love. Consequently, the lover must love the loved one until he or she learns how to love the lover back.

The truth of the matter is that God loved me first, and it took me a while to learn how to reciprocate as best I could. To understand that, we need look no further than the fact that if you find yourself in a season of rebellion, in a season of doing whatever you're led to do in your carnality, God is saying to you that he really wants a relationship with you. Even if you're choosing the path of death, he is offering life. While you choose chaos, he offers reset. While the Enemy desires to kill, steal, and destroy, we know that God came in Christ that we might have life and have it more abundantly.

> Love is never defined by the one who is loved. It is defined by the lover.

God is calling you out of the madness. God is calling you to the quality of life that he has designed for you from the very beginning. He really wants this to work.

Hosea and Gomer

Perhaps no better example exists of the kind of love God is offering than that found as we unpack the life of the minor prophet Hosea. Hosea prophesied during a period of extreme moral decline, when people had turned to their idols and mixed them in with their worship of the one true God. Even the priests had turned away from what God had called them to do. And yet God continued to prove his steadfast love in the midst of their rebellion and disobedience. He did so through Hosea, using the prophet's own life to dramatize the reality of God's love of his people.

God told Hosea, "Go take yourself a wife of harlotry and children of harlotry, for the land has committed great harlotry by departing from the LORD" (Hosea 1:2). It was as if God sent his prophet to the red-light district to seek a wife.

Her name was Gomer. And Hosea, this anointed man with the word of God on his lips, saw the woman God had sent to him to marry. Picture the ancient version of stiletto heels, fishnet stockings, and a miniskirt. She was wearing too much lipstick and a gaudy wig, and she was walking from one car to the next, from trick to trick.

God told the prophet, "That's the one I want to be your wife."

Hosea, maintaining his honor and dignity as best he could, had to stand up and proclaim, "Gomer, God has sent me to be your husband." Think about the men standing around, some of whom had no doubt been with her, making fun of him, saying, "You can't be talking about her!" But Hosea was on assignment from God, and he was there to take her as his bride and prove that he really loved her.

You can picture it: They married, and Hosea took Gomer home, cleaned her up, and gave her something good to eat. The first few days were wonderful, but then late one night, those streets started calling her name again. Gomer slipped back into her miniskirt and fishnets and went back out into the red-light district.

Hosea woke in the middle of the night and discovered her missing. He got up and went down to the red-light district wearing a sandwich board that said, "If anybody sees my Gomer, tell her I'll be right here waiting on her. Tell her I love her."

By this time, the guys on the street corner were joined by passersby, shopkeepers, cops—everybody. Word had spread. People knew Hosea and Gomer, and they knew the score. They walked by Hosea and laughed. "You've lost your mind," they said. "She's back on the streets. She'll never love you like you love her." But yet he said, "Tell her that I'll be right here when she finally decides to come home."

Hosea waited for her night after night until finally, early one morning, she stumbled in. She had one broken-heeled shoe in her hand, and she was bloody and battered. What did Hosea do? He welcomed her and loved on her again. He made her some breakfast and told her, "I want you to know that no matter what you've done during the night, I still love you. I'm still committed to this relationship."

Tell Them How Much I Love Them

I know that you may be shaking your head. You can't begin to comprehend spending a night as Hosea did, much less years. You're saying, "There's no way I could be like him." That may well be true. Only a few of us really have the capacity to be Hosea, to love like that. But all of us have been Gomer. We are all wicked by nature. We have done what we wanted to do. We all have run from God.

The good news is that God doesn't give up on us—even when we have given up on ourselves. Hosea's relationship with Gomer is a picture of God's relationship with Israel and his relationship with us. Its message is that God really wants this relationship to work. He knows that, as with Gomer, there will come a day when you get sick and tired of being sick and tired. You will come to realize where your real help comes from, and you'll choose to fall into the arms of someone who really loves you rather than into the hands of those who continuously abuse you.

The good news is that God doesn't give up on us—even when we have given up on ourselves.

"Tell them," said God to Hosea, "just how much I love them. Show them with your life." Through Hosea, he pleaded with his people, who were just like Gomer, to return.

Here is an authentic call back to relationship with God. The world has robbed you. The world has hurt you. The world has mishandled you. The world did not understand you. But God wants relationship with you. God is calling us to turn back to him.

The idea of repentance is really saying, "God, I've gone too far. I'm ready to turn around and get my life back together." That is the essence of reset. Israel recognized that the punishment they were experiencing was the result of not being what God wanted them to be. It is up to us to recognize that we are in need of authentic relationship with God and to seek that relationship.

It is not simply a matter of going to church. There are some people who attend just because they've been told it's the right thing to do. There are others who come because a family member is pressuring them, and still others who come out of form and fashion. What we are seeking instead is an organic, authentic relationship with God, the kind where you wake up in the morning saying, "This is the day the LORD has made. [I] will rejoice and be glad in it" (Ps. 118:24). It is a relationship in which you give God glory, no matter where you are, where nobody has to force you to come to church, and nobody has to force you to talk about how much you love God because when you think about what God has done in your life, you can't keep it to yourself.

You want a relationship that is not a hobby, not a plaything. You want one that is real, through and through. That is what reset gives us—a real relationship with God. And once we return, God has promised healing. Your

That is what reset gives us—a real relationship with God.

disobedience has torn you, but he will heal you. Your sin has caused you to be smitten, but he will bind you.

Pain and Healing

It's worth taking a closer look at the pain that can lead us to reset. The kind of pain experienced by Gomer was no doubt severe, for no one can live in rebellion and long escape its lasting effect. But there is a duality in all of our pain. Much of it is caused by evil. We acquiesce to temptation toward the things that cause pain and suffer the consequences.

We understand that pain, for we know we participated in it and we know we deserved it. Still, its lingering effects can cause bitterness and hardness in our spirits. We are wounded by unhealthy relationships, and we struggle with the anger that grows out of the pain, but the reality is that God says, "It doesn't matter what happened to you. I can still bind you up. I can take away the pain. I can heal a broken heart. I can repair a jaded mind." Whatever it is, God can make it right.

God sometimes allows you to be hurt by people or situations where you are not at fault. *How is that possible?* you think. *Why would God allow pain to come my way?* Many of us simply get angry at God and turn against him in moments like that. But that pain, like the pain that grows out of our rebellious actions, is in reality a gift from God. He is saying, in essence, "I am doing this in order to help you." Just as it takes pain to teach us to avoid hot stoves and other causes of physical injury, it takes pain to teach us the limits of behavior, people, or situations that can hurt us mentally, emotionally, and spiritually. It is there to push us away from danger. That is the positive side of pain.

At times God acts like a skilled surgeon who realizes that some healing will never take place unless a cut is made. A knife in a skilled surgeon's hand is sometimes the only thing standing between a patient and death. The surgeon's object is not to hurt the patient, although he knows you will experience pain, but to heal. Without that cut, the cancer, the infection, the damaged organ would never be treated.

That is what God is doing with you. He knows the cut he is making hurts you, but he knows it is the gateway to healing and wholeness. And God, as the ultimate skilled surgeon, can stitch you together again so that when you heal, there will be no scars. "Come, and let us return to the LORD; for He has torn, but He will heal us; He has stricken, but He will bind us up" (Hosea 6:1).

Think of the times when God had to cut you and your reaction was, "Lord, it just isn't fair." But now, when you look back over your life, you thank God for the surgery since it took things out of you that were not good for you. Some of you would still be in unhealthy relationships if God had not performed that

> God, as the ultimate skilled surgeon, can stitch you together again so that when you heal, there will be no scars.

surgery, and in many cases God healed you without scars. So many of us now can say, "That stuff I was crying over ten years ago I'm laughing at today."

But, being human, we often rush right into another bad relationship, another unproductive situation. When God uses a fresh cut, renewed pain, to get us out, we're again crying the night away. That's the time to remember what has happened before, to realize that this is something you'll get through. You will get over the pain, and maybe this time you'll learn the lesson he wants you to learn.

Divine Resuscitation

This lesson of divine resuscitation appears many times in the Bible. Deuteronomy 32:39 says, "Now see that I, even I, am He, and there is no God besides Me; I kill and I make alive; I wound and I heal." Jeremiah 30:17 says, "For I will restore health to you and heal you of your wounds." God is saying, "And when I get through healing you, I'm going to position you for revival." And that is in essence what reset is—a revival for one.

God even lays out the process. After Hosea 6:1, in which he promises healing, we read, "After two days He will revive us" (v. 2). It's important that we understand the continuity. God provides space between the incision and the next move. He is telling us not to move too quickly. Give God time to heal you. Don't bounce, as so many do, from one thing to the next. That was Gomer's problem as well. You keep bouncing from one car to the next, from one smile to the next, from one relationship to the next. Give yourself time to heal before God's next move.

> *After two days He will revive us;*
> *On the third day He will raise us up,*
> *That we may live in His sight.* (v. 2)

God is getting ready to take you through the process of resuscitation. As sure as Lazarus rose from the dead, you can rise from where you are. Whatever is dead in your life—marriage, friendships, job, money, morale—is about to experience a revival that's going to bring spiritual life back into you. You may have lost the pep in your step. You may have lost the passion that brings dreams to fruition in your life. You may have lost your desire for the things of God. But God promises spiritual CPR, divine resuscitation—a word that means "to raise up again," although we use it to mean "to bring around," to bring back from unconsciousness to consciousness. CPR is the process of getting your heart beating and getting the breath of life into your lungs. That is the power of reset.

When God made Adam, Adam was not a living being until God blew his breath into him. The Hebrew word for "breath" and for "spirit" is *ruach*, a word whose very pronunciation pushes air from your lips. That *whoosh*, that *ruach*, is what God breathed into Adam. It is the very breath that Jesus gave up on the cross when his spirit returned to the Father in heaven. It is the breath, the wind that came from the corners of the earth in Ezekiel 37, over the dried, disjointed bones in the desert, to cause them to stand up like a mighty army. And it is the same breath that God's Spirit breathes into you.

Get Up!

God is ready to speak, to breathe, to blow over everything that is dead in your life. He is about to *whoosh* all over your situation! He's about to *whoosh* over your marriage, your career, your schoolwork. He is about to send a fresh wind over your home and your family. Ask the Lord to breathe over every aspect of your life, and he will.

It's one thing to be resuscitated. It's another to get up. And Ephesians 2:4–6 says,

> But God, who is rich in mercy, because of His great love with which He loved us, even when we were dead in trespasses, made us alive together with Christ (by grace you have been saved), and raised us up together and made us sit together in the heavenly places in Christ Jesus.

[God] is about to send a fresh wind over your home and your family.

When we make the decision to repent and turn from our wicked ways, God quickens us and raises us up together to sit with our elder brother, Christ Jesus.

Getting up, in a sense this profound—for this is, after all, coming to life after spiritual death—means a completely new countenance. No longer will you wallow in a dead place around dead people. You will be radiating life. "Stop looking like you're dead," God is saying. "Look alive! I am changing your posture, your position. Stop making excuses as to why you must stay down. Get up!"

Get up out of that place of craziness. Get out of that place of abuse. Get out of that place of exploitation. Get up and be who God has called you to be. Live in such a way that those who wrote you off as dead will have to take back everything.

God offers faithfulness and promises restoration. Gomer represents Israel. Israel represents us. God says, "Come on back home. I love you. I've been standing here waiting on you. I saw you out there doing what you were doing, but come on back. I'm going to love you even when I ought to leave you alone. When you get sick and tired of being sick and tired, I'll be right here loving on you, waiting on you to come back home. I'm going to clean you up. I'm going to give you position. I'm going to remind you of who you are and I'm going to heal you of all your wounds, all the stuff that happened to you when you were out there, all the pain. I am going to raise you up to a level where people won't even know it's you."

Rain and Revelation

Let's keep going. In this part of Hosea, God is saying, "I'm getting ready to reset you in a way that's about to blow your mind."

Hosea 6:3 says,

> *Let us know,*
> *Let us pursue the knowledge of the* LORD.
> *His going forth is established as the morning;*
> *He will come to us like the rain,*
> *Like the latter and former rain to the earth.*

There is a distinction between *information* about God and *revelation* about God. Information is cognitive. It's what you read in a book. It's based on your intellect. Revelation is based on your spirit and your experiences. I know people with plenty of book sense who have no common sense. I know people who are intellectually brilliant but spiritually dim, who have no idea how God is moving in this season. That's something you can't find in a textbook. When God is moving in your life, it isn't your intellect that responds. When you get a revelation of God, it is not based on information but on what you've been through. When you've seen God preserve you and keep you from losing your mind, when God has kept you together while everything around you is falling apart, you recognize that it's revelation, something that lives within. It's revelation that gives me a breakthrough when I should have had a breakdown.

God is saying, "I'm getting ready to reset you in a way that's about to blow your mind."

Revelation, when you feel it and when you live it, will make sense to you, but it may not make sense to the people around you. The other courtiers in the court of the Persian king could not know what Esther knew. Hosea could not expect those around him to understand his love for Gomer. But whether or not other people get it, it is important for you to get it, and to hold on to it. God is about to reset you, but you cannot look for others to understand. It is something you understand in faith and through experience.

God's providence, his movement in us and through us, is as established as morning. When you, as Gomer, look over your life, ask yourself: Has there ever been a day you've been alive that morning has not come? And if the morning comes, doesn't it come with the promise of a new beginning, a second chance, a third chance, a fourth or a fifth? It doesn't matter how long and dark and painful the night was, Gomer, or what you did in the dark. "Weeping may endure for a night," says Psalm 30:5, "but joy comes in the morning."

Gomer, someone exploited you. Someone told you what to do. But it's time to say good-bye to everyone and everything that exploited you. It's time to let Jesus love you. It's time to give God glory for healing you without scars, for cleaning you up and straightening you out. He has filled you and he is about to take you into another dimension. There is more to come, whether it has to do with your marriage, your relationships, your friendships, your job, your money, or your health. Tell the doubters that you have gotten your revelation, that it is inside you and more real than any book knowledge.

God is about to turn this thing around. Don't wait until the battle is won. Lift your hands and praise him.

Jesus, My Choice

If, like Gomer, you have been delivered from evil, I am calling you to show it! If you're going to be for God, act like it! If you're going to be for God, walk like it! If you're going to be for God, talk like it! Say:

- I'm choosing faith over fear.
- I'm choosing worship over worry.
- I'm choosing love over loneliness.
- I'm choosing grace over guilt.
- I'm choosing peace over possessions.
- I'm choosing praise over pouting.
- I'm choosing goodness over gloom.
- I'm choosing mercy over misery.
- I'm choosing salvation over sin.
- I'm choosing heaven over hell.

REFLECTIONS

- What stands in your way as a Christian?
- What missions might God have in store for you as he calls you to reset?
- Who are the role models in your life, people you might call on as you reset?
- Are you ready to celebrate your reset, to demonstrate the life you've reentered?

CHAPTER 3

RECOGNIZE THE CALL

It's time to get it together. Each of us has an inner voice that has said that at one time or another. You may be hearing it right now. Your position in life is irrelevant. The tuned-in, well-connected young professional can feel the tug just as surely as the lonely retiree. At some point each of us comes to that place where we know it's time to change course.

Listen carefully, and you'll recognize the call for what it is—an urging of the Spirit. It is sometimes gentle, sometimes in your face, but this is what it is saying: *Now is the time to move. Start doing what God has called you to do.*

Jonah heard it. Abram and Moses heard it, and so did many others whom we will meet in the course of reading this book. There is no higher calling than living out the destiny God has for us, and we are talking in this book about how to get on board with that call. This is about getting

Start doing what God has called you to do. back to when we were new in the Lord, with that fresh-from-the-factory shine and a heart burning to learn about and serve God. It's about clearing away the cobwebs, getting back to that place where we are untarnished and undefeated.

Remember that place? It's where you were when you were so passionate about God that there was nothing downtown or on television or online that could take the place of reading his Word late into the night, no one had to beg you to worship God, and no one had to prompt you to sing his praises. It was where you were before the pains of living and the temptations of the world came between you and God.

Maybe you've never really been to that place, but you can almost feel, deep down in your marrow, what it must be like to be there. You know that spiritual riches the likes of which you've never known can be yours if only you will get back inside the will of God. This book is your treasure map, with a practical plan for getting there, for experiencing a relationship with God that lights the fires of passion within you and lets you become precisely the person he wants you to be.

We are not talking minor tweaks. This is a period in history when there are so many distractions, so many ways to get off course that, for most of us, getting back to where we need to be involves drastic, profound change. What we need is a reset.

Life Outside God's Will

Let's look at the symptoms that show when we are outside God's will. They're the unmistakable signs that God's riches have eluded us. They are the things that cry out for reset.

Emptiness. So many people feel there is something missing, that the things that occupy them day in and day out don't add up to a life that is truly worthwhile and meaningful.

Lack of Direction. Many people are simply unsure of how to set their rudders. They are unable to choose sound priorities from life's many possibilities.

Lack of Control. Sometimes life is moving too fast. Our schedules, families, and jobs feel like foreign entities that buffet us about. We begin to feel like spokes in someone else's wheel.

Frustration. This is the feeling that fills us when who we are and what we've become don't match who we'd like to be and what we should be.

Fear. This emotion can overwhelm us. It may be fear of the future, fear of entering into or losing a relationship, fear of taking that next big step, fear of failing—or even fear of succeeding.

The common thread here? *Meaning.* When we are living without a sense of meaning, when we don't feel like part of a plan, negativity and disorientation follow. And it's clear that we are unable to make life meaningful on our own. That takes God.

The good news is that for all its power, for all the hold it has on many of us, the world is no match for God, and there is something powerful taking place that each of us can be a part of. In its large form it is termed *revival*. On an individual basis it is the reset we are talking about.

You are not reading this book by accident. Maybe you have already sensed a shift in the spiritual atmosphere. Maybe you have begun to reflect on your life, on what disobedience and worldliness have cost you. Maybe you have already sensed the amazing things God has in store for you and have begun to look at how the devil has done his best to rob you of it. Maybe you're at the point where you're willing to say, "I will do whatever it takes. I am ready to enter the kingdom God has already prepared for me."

> The good news is that for all its power, for all the hold it has on many of us, the world is no match for God.

Has it been a while since you've shaken off the dust, put a shine on, and stepped out with God? Do you need a reset? Does your marriage? Your job? Your relationship with your family? Your ego? Your outlook on life? Then you are in the right place. Let's walk together through the steps each of us can take to reset ourselves, to rejoin God in the journey toward our proper destiny.

We will now look at Mephibosheth and Jonah, two people whose stories explore two sides of the reset coin.

Mephibosheth had nothing and was called to the king's table. Jonah had everything, and nearly threw it all away en route to a new sense of purpose. Let's look at what they can teach us.

Mephibosheth: Called Out of Barrenness

> So David said to him, "Do not fear, for I will surely show you kindness for Jonathan your father's sake, and will restore to you all the land of Saul your grandfather; and you shall eat bread at my table continually." . . . But Mephibosheth your master's son shall eat bread at my table always.
>
> —2 SAMUEL 9:7, 10

Many of us are in situations that make us feel constricted. We feel like others are walling us in and trying to limit us. Sometimes the culprit is obvious—a boss, a company, an overbearing relative or friend. Sometimes, though, it's someone who means us nothing but good. Many parents smother their children with dreams and goals that don't take into account the child's talents and interests. Misguided teachers and coaches sometimes box young people in as they try to mold them or push them. Unfortunately, even the church doesn't always create enough space for people. There are rules, regulations, and restrictions that have more to do with the convenience of those who make them than the protection of those bound by them. In some cases, those restrictions can marginalize, stigmatize, and even ostracize people. They push them to the periphery, beyond the chance for reconciliation.

Every believer should realize that regardless of where you are, no matter what context or situation you find yourself in, God is ready to manifest his plan in your life. If you have a dream that is of God, he will always give you the space to reach for it. He will encourage you to give your best. Adversity is no stumbling block. Nothing can prevent the will of God from coming to fruition. No devil in hell can stop him.

If you have a dream that is of God, he will always give you the space to reach for it.

We will look here at the story of Mephibosheth, whose story is told in 2 Samuel. Whether or not you are already familiar with him, his plight should have a familiar ring. We meet him in a place called Lo Debar. It is a place of rejection and ambiguity, a place people put you when they don't know quite what to do with you. It is a place where you are misunderstood and often mislabeled.

In Hebrew, *Lo Debar* means "no pasture" or "no word." This is a place without green grass—something common enough in the Middle East. There is no vegetation, no life. This is fruitless land, a place of barrenness. To add insult to injury, this is a place where there is no word. There is no revelation to be had.

A lot of people today find themselves living or working

in Lo Debar. It can inhabit your spirit and fill your mind. You may be in a relationship that places you in Lo Debar. Or perhaps you have moved on and you encounter Lo Debar when you revisit old friends or your old neighborhood. Sometimes people put you in Lo Debar by attaching names to you that permanently define you as the one who's outside. They may exaggerate truths or spread falsehoods. They often do that without a real understanding of who you are or how you got to be where you are in life. They don't know your story, but they make assumptions.

It is just as true that many of us place ourselves in Lo Debar. Our mistakes, our assumptions, our arrogance or, conversely, our self-doubt may place us there.

But I am here to tell you that no matter how you got there, and no matter how dismal things may appear, Lo Debar can be the setting for your greatest turnaround. You may experience your greatest breakthrough there, for God has the power to meet you in Lo Debar and turn your situation around. Others may mock or pity you once they decide you are in Lo Debar, but they will come to learn that God is going to have the last laugh.

My ministry is in part about pulling people out of this place of victimization. It is about turning victims into victors. As we look at the story of Mephibosheth, keep in mind that you don't have to live in Lo Debar, and if you do, you don't have to remain there. God has the power and capacity to assure you that Lo Debar will not be your final destination. He can bring you to a place of blessing unlike any you can imagine, so that your life coming out of Lo Debar looks nothing like your life when you went in.

Understanding Why We Are in Lo Debar

After years in hiding and years of battle, David came to the throne as the anointed king. In those days, a transition of power and authority in Israel meant the incoming king could do what he wanted with those from the old regime. In fact, it was customary simply to annihilate all those who were in allegiance with the deposed king.

David, though, had felt great love for Jonathan, the son of former King Saul. Both had died, Jonathan in combat, Saul of suicide. When David took power, he wondered, given all the bloodshed, "Is there still anyone left of the house of Saul, that I may show him kindness for Jonathan's sake?" (2 Samuel 9:1 ESV).

Notice he did not ask, "Is there anybody qualified for kindness?" or "Is there anyone worthy of kindness?" He simply wondered whether there was anyone left in the house of Saul to whom he could direct kindness.

Ziba, the king's servant, came and said to David, "There is one."

"Who is he?" said David.

Ziba told him of Mephibosheth, Jonathan's son, and told him where he lived in Lo Debar. He added the detail that Mephibosheth was "lame in his feet" (v. 3). David told Ziba he wanted to see Mephibosheth, and Ziba went off to look for him.

If we understand why Mephibosheth was in Lo Debar, that place of barrenness, we might understand better how you and I come to be in places that are inconsistent with God's will for our lives. Mephibosheth's dilemma was rooted in his paralysis. The Bible says that Mephibosheth was a boy of five when news came to the palace that Jonathan and Saul, Mephibosheth's father and grandfather, were dead. The nurse attending Mephibosheth wanted to save him from whatever calamity might come to the palace, and so she grabbed him and fled. As she was running, she fell, and Mephibosheth fell with her. Most likely he broke bones in his feet or ankles that never healed correctly, and he was rendered lame the rest of his life. He was never able to progress at the pace God had intended for his life because someone got distracted and dropped him.

At the point where we meet him, Mephibosheth was living in less-than-ideal circumstances. Then Ziba came to him saying, "The king wants to see you."

A Place of Isolation

Like Mephibosheth, when you are in a place of loneliness or fear, God knows it. He is aware whenever you are in a position where you are categorized, where you are called "other." It could be physical. It could be emotional or mental. He knows the cause as well.

In the case of Mephibosheth, this misfortune could not be attributed to his own actions. His paralysis and stagnation grew directly out of the actions of someone else. That may be the case for you as well. There are many conditions you can attest to that are the result of things you've done to yourself, but then there are things that have happened to you because of someone else's carelessness in your life. Many of us have injuries, physical or psychological, that were caused by the actions of others, either intentionally or not. All of us know what it's like to be dropped by someone

When you are in a place of loneliness or fear, God knows it.

else: Someone made you a promise but then dropped you. Someone abused you and then dropped you. Somebody did you wrong and then dropped you. Those injuries may have induced paralysis of one sort or another in you. You are unable to progress at the pace that God intends for your life.

So many people struggle today with some kind of paralysis. It could be a marriage that is at a standstill. It could be the inability to handle money. It could be a dysfunctional relationship. Emotionally and spiritually, there are many ways to be lame, to be crippled by the past. There are many ways to enter Lo Debar.

Once you are in Lo Debar, the people who put you there may want to keep you there. They must create a place that reinforces and reaffirms what you have been called, to remind you that you are the different one because if they don't, you might well wake up and realize your real name, your true identity. But until then, every day you wake up, you are reminded that you're the one who will never get out of this situation.

Lo Debar is a dismal place. It is a place of isolation, a place where you can be around a lot of people but still feel isolated. It's a place where nobody, not even those closest to you, understands the depth of your pain or what you're going through. Once that isolation settles in, there is an interrogation, the point at which the enemy says, "What's wrong with you? Why don't you have this? Why don't you have that? God must not love you. Look, you can't move. You're a paralytic. You have lameness in your legs. Everybody else is moving on. Why isn't it happening for you? Everybody else is getting married. Why isn't it happening for you? Everybody else is graduating. Why isn't it happening for you? Everybody else is paying their bills. Why isn't it happening for you?"

Once the enemy takes up residence in your head, that kind of negative introspection can cause you to spiral even further. If there's anything I've learned, though, it's that you have a choice. You can go through a breakdown, or you can declare, "I'm going to get a breakthrough." You have to make up your mind. You have to say you're not going to let these thoughts mess with your mind. You're not going to let the enemy make you believe that God has given up on you.

You Are About To Be Discovered

In the midst of the greatest frustrations, during the most oppressive moments of your life, God can step in, as David did with Mephibosheth, and give you a promise—you are about to be discovered.

Ziba showed up looking for Mephibosheth at just the right time, in just the right place. When it's your time, God will do whatever is necessary to bring it to pass. God knows exactly where you are. You don't have to pass out your business card. You don't have to say, "Here I am, God." He knows your address. He knows the tears you've cried. He knows the times you've been up all night long. Your Ziba is the messenger who shows up and tells your spirit, "I have come with a word from the king." Your Ziba may be the man or woman in church who gives you a word, the neighbor who reminds you of your worth, the news story that impresses upon you how deeply we all are connected, the passage in the Bible that spells out God's promise.

> In the midst of the greatest frustrations, during the most oppressive moments of your life, God can step in . . . and give you a promise.

But you can't hear God's call if you are too self-absorbed, if you hurry in and out of church and don't speak to anybody, if you act as if you already know it all. The fact is that you don't know where that word telling you something is about to happen in your life is going to come from.

Somebody you haven't met yet may well be coming to bless you. You have to be ready, as Mephibosheth was.

Lo Debar is by no means where you want to stay. It is not ideal. It is not conducive to fruitfulness. It is a place of aridity, depression, and despair. It is frustrating and irritating. And yet there may come a moment in your life when God won't let you leave your bad situation quite yet because he says your next breakthrough will not come in a place of ease and comfort. It is going to come right there in that place you've been trying to get out of. That's why you can't let weariness overtake you.

The King Wants to See You

Often the kind of paralysis we face is one of attitude. We become lethargic. We act defeated. We stop believing in ourselves and our dreams. God promises that in due season, you're going to reap, but if you faint now, you won't see the breakthrough. You must stay there until it comes, until you can clearly hear the king's voice. They may not like you on the job, but stay there. They may roll their eyes at you, but stay there. Hang in there until the breakthrough shows up. Mephibosheth waited, and Ziba showed up, coming into Lo Debar. In this place with no word, Ziba showed up with a word.

"The king wants to see you," Zilba said. *The king wants to see you.* Are there any more powerful words? When Mephibosheth heard that invitation, he did not ask, "What do you think I should do? Do you think I should go with this man?" He knew this call came from the king. He knew Ziba represented release.

When you've been in barren, bitter Lo Debar long enough, and you finally get a word, you couldn't care less what people think about it. You pack your bags and get your stuff together and you say, "I'm out of here. This is my last day in Lo Debar." And by the way, if this was an earthly king, if this was the president and he summoned you, wouldn't you be certain to go? Why should you be any less eager or compelled to go when the King of kings is calling you to reset?

Verse 5 says, "King David sent and brought him out of the house of Machir the son of Ammiel, from Lo Debar."

We often forget verse 6, and it's one we need to remember: when Mephibosheth reached David, "he fell on his face and prostrated himself." Too many of us come before the king standing up. When we are called by the King, we should come before him in a spirit of humility that reflects that we know we need him. He offers something no human can offer. He brings healing no medicine can bring. He has power no official can match. And God wants us to acknowledge that we need what only the King can give.

And so, David said, "Mephibosheth?" And he answered, "Here is your servant!" (v. 6).

David said, "Do not fear." He knew Mephibosheth was thinking there was a good chance he was simply going to be slaughtered, since he was part of the old regime. David had every right to do that. But, said David, "I will surely show you kindness for Jonathan your father's sake, and will restore to you all the land of Saul your grandfather; and you shall eat bread at my table continually" (2 Samuel 9:7).

[God] offers something no human can offer.

Mephibosheth bowed down and said, "What is your servant, that you should look upon such a dead dog as I?" (v. 8). Nobody had ever told Mephibosheth of his worth. He had been awakened every morning for years and told he was the crippled one and treated as such. He was the one who had been dropped. Nobody reminded him of his legacy. Nobody told him of his bloodline. He was just five when his father died, and he probably had only vague memories, if any. It seems no one treated him like someone who had once been royalty, as he had been—and you *are*, if you have been redeemed.

Greatness in Your Blood

Cicero once said, "To know nothing of what happened before you were born is to remain a child forever." There is a generation of us who know nothing of where we've come from, and you will never reach your destiny if you don't know your history. Mephibosheth was in that position. He referred to himself as a "dead dog." He was unable to embrace what God was about to do in this life. He had been poisoned by a culture that had spit venom into his life, speaking negativity to him and shattering his self-esteem.

Are you in that position today? Do you come to church week after week hearing the Word of God proclaim your awesome destiny yet see yourself as a dead dog? Do you live in a context where people are telling you you're not going to have anything and you're not going to be anything? Have you allowed your self-esteem to be so messed up that the picture you see of yourself is all wrong?

You have vision. You have dreams. What's more, you have greatness in your blood. You have destiny in your lineage. It doesn't matter who rejects you or who labels you. You are God's child. God gave Abraham a promise, telling him, "Out of your seed, every nation is going to be blessed," and Jesus Christ is of the bloodline of Abraham. When I got saved, when you got saved, by the blood of Jesus Christ, you and I became part of the family. Just as Mephibosheth is a part of the house of Jonathan and Saul, you are part of the house of Abraham and Jesus.

You should be able to say, "I'm sorry if you hate on me, but it's in my blood to be blessed. I won't walk with my head down."

> You have greatness in your blood. You have destiny in your lineage.

You can tell when people don't know who they are. It's easy to see when they don't know their identity, their destiny. It's in their posture. They are despondent, always walking with their heads down. Walk with your head up, with your shoulders square. Let people call you stuck up. Let them say, "You think you're all that." Say, "I *am* all that! I am what God says I am. Why do you want me walking around depressed and broken and pitiful? That's not my testimony!"

God sent you here. God has a glorious plan for you. God wants to change your destiny.

Mephibosheth went from Lo Debar, the place of no pasture, no word, to Jerusalem and the king's table, just like that.

I have no logical explanation for it. I have no theological thesis to argue. I have no philosophical rationale for how this happened and how it continues to happen. All I can tell you is that when God gets ready to bless you, he can do it—just like that.

Out of Lo Debar

Your destiny under God's plan does not depend on your past. The person you were ten years or one year or six weeks or twenty-four hours ago does not define who you are in this moment. Tell yourself, "I don't have to be this broke. I don't have to be this depressed. God is about to lift me out of here, out of Lo Debar." Maybe you've been rejected; maybe you've been dejected. Maybe you've been forgotten; maybe you've struggled. Or maybe you've been wounded. People have lied to you and about you. People have consigned you to a place where they thought they could define you. I come to declare what Psalm 75:6–7 says,

For not from the east or from the west
and not from the wilderness comes lifting up,
but it is God who executes judgment,
putting down one and lifting up another. (ESV)

Those people judging you are not the ones who matter. They do not determine your destiny. God is going to bring you to the king's table. It doesn't matter what *has* happened in your life. Something awesome is *about to* happen. It may have been rough. You may have felt like giving up. But God is calling you out of Lo Debar. Get ready. God is saying, "Your time has come. The king wants to see you. I come to snatch you out of Lo Debar. I come to pull you out of that place of depression. I come to pull you out of that place the enemy wants to keep you. I come to help you reclaim the destiny the enemy has been trying to rob you of."

Your destiny under God's plan does not depend on your past.

Whether your own actions or the actions of others placed you in Lo Debar, I am here to tell you the king is pulling people out of this place of victimization and making them victors. You do not have to live in this place. Mephibosheth did not ask anyone for permission. When the king wants to see you, you have to go.

Come out of Lo Debar, however you can. I'm not sure how Mephibosheth made it to Jerusalem to reach the king. He couldn't walk. But when you need a breakthrough, you'll crawl; you'll find someone to carry you; you'll do whatever you have to do.

Drop your excuses. Come before the king. Accept that the Lord is about to turn your life around. Keep telling yourself, "I am not going to let Lo Debar break me." Believe and come before him. You have an appointment with the king. Come out of that place of despair and accept your place at his table.

Jonah: Resisting the Call

How do we know we've been called to reset? Often the first credible evidence is that we face resistance. God doesn't call us to easy. He calls us to hard. We are taking his light and his message into a world that often doesn't want to hear what we have to say.

But the resistance generally starts before the world even knows—it begins in our own heads and hearts. Let's look at the case of Jonah, whose story any of us can understand. He heard the call, "Arise, go to Nineveh, that great city, and cry out against it; for their wickedness has come up before Me" (Jonah 1:2).

Nineveh was the capital of the Assyrian Kingdom. It was in modern-day Iraq, five hundred miles east of Jonah's hometown in present-day Israel. So what did Jonah do? He got on a ship headed for Tarshish, which was more than two thousand miles in the other direction, near Gibraltar. He wanted to be as far from Nineveh as he could get!

Why? The Assyrians were enemies of Israel and Jonah

didn't want to take the chance that they'd repent and be spared. He wanted to see them slaughtered, so he ran away.

His journey has lessons for us. First, you'll notice that it isn't hard to find people willing to carry you *away* from the will of God. Bad companions are everywhere. What's more, running has a price. Buying passage from Joppa all the way across the Mediterranean wasn't cheap. Then, being outside God's will invites storms, and Jonah and his shipmates were soon in the midst of a big one.

Jonah teaches us a major lesson here. When you find yourself in a storm, whether it's within a relationship, at work, or among your friends, look at yourself first. If you're outside the will of God, you may well be the problem. Jonah figured out pretty quickly that the problem on this particular ship was him.

When you find yourself in a storm . . . look at yourself first. If you're outside the will of God, you may well be the problem.

"Pick me up and hurl me into the sea," he told his shipmates. "Then the sea will quiet down for you" (v. 12 ESV).

Little did Jonah realize that he was about to be reset. It turned out that the calamity he faced—being thrown from a warm ship (it was comfortable enough that he had been asleep when the storm began) into the cold waters of the sea—was actually a blessing. Being tossed overboard released Jonah to his destiny. God had, after all, prepared a great fish to swallow him and transport him. And God's planning had been personalized and meticulous.

The fish was the right size and, more importantly, it was in the right place.

Provision and Opportunity

God will send us opportunities to get back into his will, even when we are running from it. And he will send provision even when it doesn't look that way.

Maybe you were fired. Maybe you've been dumped. Maybe your financial situation looks dire. But you are alive, and the fact that you're reading this book means you're searching, that you're open to God's voice. Your calamity may simply be God's way of releasing you to your destiny. Rest assured, he has prepared a place to hold you and transport you back into his will.

Maybe, like Jonah's place inside the fish, it will feel dark and cramped. You may be cut off from friends and family. You may be outside a church community. Like Jonah, you may have no one to turn to but God. No friend, no loved one, can offer you what you need. There's no one at the other end of your cell phone or computer who can lift you out of the hole you're in.

But if you have cried out to the Lord, as Jonah did, you can bet you are being ferried to the exact latitude and longitude where God wants you to be. God has prepared your great fish. The Lord kept Jonah safe until he regained his senses and cried out to the Lord. At that moment, he was reset.

Once Jonah said yes to the Lord, the fish "vomited out Jonah upon the dry land" (2:10 KJV). His yes—the fact that he had gotten back into the Lord's will—became an irritant to the fish. Certain places and things aren't equipped to handle righteousness. When you say yes, when you start praying, you will get tossed back onto dry land by your good-time friends who are not interested in someone who is running *toward* God. A reset will place you on solid ground.

Now, that's not to say you'll be pretty when you get to the beach. Jonah certainly wasn't. You may well be covered in the things that were in the fish's belly. Jonah, after all, complained about the seaweed clinging to his head. But such things are, in reality, the vestiges of disobedience.

Still, God uses people who are covered in vomit. He uses people with scars and old wounds. Those are sometimes the very things that give your story credibility, that show people that you were not then what you are now.

And like Jonah, who finally led Nineveh to salvation, you will be more useful because of your past, because of those scars, because of the things God has called you out of, once you have been reset.

REFLECTIONS

- Do life's distractions sometimes stand between you and God?
- What is your Lo Debar? How does living there affect you?

- Are you running toward or from God's will?
- Describe a time in your life when an apparent calamity actually released you toward your destiny and allowed a greater good to take place.

CHAPTER 4

REASSESS AND RECALIBRATE

So when he had received food, he was strengthened.
Then Saul spent some days with the disciples at
Damascus. Immediately he preached the Christ in
the synagogues, that He is the Son of God. Then
all who heard were amazed, and said, "Is this not
he who destroyed those who called on this name
in Jerusalem, and has come here for that purpose,
so that he might bring them bound to the chief
priests?"

—ACTS 9:19–21

Want to see reset at its rawest and most powerful? Let's talk
about Saul of Tarsus. His reset turned a violent enemy of the
young church into its most effective advocate and the author
of a third of the New Testament—the apostle Paul.

I meet many people all the time who think their sins, their past, and the trail of wreckage strewn behind them place them beyond hope and out of the reach of Jesus. Their reputations, they think, are set in stone. They're afraid that even if they were to accept Jesus and become part of his church, those who know them would still see them as the same sinners they've always been.

They have nothing on Saul. Neither have you. This is the man who watched over the cloaks of those who stoned Stephen to death. This is the man who then set about "ravaging the church, and entering house after house, he dragged off men and women and committed them to prison" (Acts 8:3 ESV). Then he set off toward Damascus, bearing letters of introduction from the high priest, Caiaphas, with plans to arrest followers of the Way, as fledgling Christianity was called at that time, and "bring them bound to Jerusalem" (9:2). Saul had blood on his hands.

While Saul was on the road to Damascus, Acts tells us he saw a brilliant light that caused him to fall to the ground.

"Saul, Saul, why are you persecuting Me?" (v. 4), said a voice.

Stunned, Saul said, "Who are You, Lord?"

"I am Jesus, whom you are persecuting" (v. 5). The voice told him to go on into Damascus, where "for three days he was without sight, and neither ate nor drank" (v. 9 ESV).

Talk about a hard reset! Saul's radical transformation changed the arc of human history. It gave the early church the missionary, teacher, and pastor who carried the Way through much of the Mediterranean, founding churches and encouraging and admonishing their members with letters that still constitute half the books of the New Testament.

As we have seen, the process of being reset begins with the call. Most of us hear that voice, although with not nearly the soul-wrenching impact that it had on Saul. We may hear it as a whisper, all but drowned out by the world and its distractions, but the call is there. It is every bit as real as Saul's, and it leaves us with the choice to pursue it or to turn away.

In Damascus the Lord called a disciple named Ananias and told him to go to the stunned and silent Saul. But Ananias knew just how hard-core Saul was. Like Jonah, Ananias didn't want any part of the Lord's invitation. But the Lord said, "Go, for he is a chosen instrument of mine to carry my name before the Gentiles and kings and the children of Israel" (v. 15 ESV). Saul received the Holy Spirit and was baptized. Then he set about making history.

You too are a chosen instrument of God! Your mission is uniquely yours, and it is every bit as real as Saul's. You can be changed, recharged, and rededicated just as profoundly, and reaching out to the church will let you find the Ananias who can help you take the next steps.

You can be changed, recharged, and rededicated.

Reset: Jacob Becomes Israel

So He said to him, "What is your name?" He said,
"Jacob." And He said, "Your name shall no longer
be called Jacob, but Israel; for you have struggled
with God and with men, and have prevailed."
—GENESIS 32:27–28

The Lord has a plan for your life. You may not see it at
the moment, but he has one for you, just as he has one for
me and for each of us. Unfortunately, far too many people
never get in tune with that plan. Some are outside the will of
God completely and never even become aware of God's plan.
Many of us recognize it early but lose track of it because we
are distracted by the things of the world.

There are also those men and women who think they
are inside the will of God when they are not. These are the
people who outwardly live the Christian life. They go to
church. They tithe. They're on committees. But so many are
guilty of working *for* God instead of *with* God. We set ourselves in motion, deciding what we think would be best for
God and God's kingdom rather than listening first for the
assignment. We are shortsighted, in that we think what *we*
want is what God wants. We think that what *we* think is
important is what *God* thinks is important. Our intentions
may be good, but unless our mission comes from God, we
may be sowing discord, doing more harm than good.

What about you? Have you drifted from God? Have

you gotten further and further from the clear understanding you once had of what God wanted? Have the passion, desire, and fervor you once had for the things of God waned? Are you operating on self-propulsion, rather than God-propulsion?

Fortunately, it is never too late to reset, whether we are off base a lot or just a little.

> Are you operating on self-propulsion, rather than God-propulsion?

Jacob's Story

Let's consider the story of Jacob, the man whose reset included a name change that to this day identifies a nation. While Saul's name change was simply a matter of his using the Roman version of his name, Paul, to become more closely identified with those to whom he was preaching, it was God who changed Jacob's name to Israel. His descendants became known as Israelites and eventually as the tribes and the kingdom of Israel.

Jacob's father, Isaac, and his mother, Rebekah, were close to the Lord. In fact, the Lord told Isaac, "I am with you and will bless you and multiply your offspring for my servant Abraham's sake" (Gen. 26:24 ESV). But you don't get credit for being the child of godly parents; God has children, not grandchildren. We are each responsible for our own relationship. We may begin that relationship thanks to our parents, or perhaps we are introduced to God through proselytization and catechism, but it is our personal experience that God uses to broaden and deepen our relationship with him.

Jacob was a trickster. The name Jacob refers to his role as a supplanter. He swindled his older twin brother out of his birthright. Then when his father was near death, Jacob teamed up with his mother to deceive him, covering himself with skins to make his father think Jacob was his hairy brother, Esau. Asked directly by Isaac whether he was really Esau, Jacob lied outright, so that he might get Esau's blessing by subterfuge. When Esau found out, he was furious, and Jacob, at his mother's behest, fled to avoid his wrath.

One night while on the run, Jacob had a dream in which God promised him and his offspring "the land on which you lie" (Gen. 28:13). He also promised that Jacob and his descendants would spread in every direction and that God would "keep you wherever you go, and will bring you back to this land" (v. 15). That convinced Jacob that the place he slept was the very "house of God . . . the gate of heaven" (v. 17).

When Jacob woke, he made a vow. "If God will be with me, and will keep me in this way that I go, and will give me bread to eat, and raiment to put on, so that I come again to my father's house in peace; then shall the LORD be my God: and this stone, which I have set for a pillar, shall be God's house: and of all that thou shalt give me I will surely give the tenth unto thee" (vv. 20–22 KJV). This was not Jacob passively accepting the God of his parents. This was Jacob in a fresh relationship based on his own experience.

Now, God takes vows very seriously. Ecclesiastes 5:4–5 says, "When you make a vow to God, do not delay to pay it; for He has no pleasure in fools. Pay what you have vowed— better not to vow than to vow and not pay."

Isaac and Rebekah had sent Jacob to Rebekah's brother, Laban, so that Jacob might marry one of his daughters. Laban tricked him into marrying two of them, Leah and Rachel, and Jacob worked for Laban for fourteen years for the privilege. When he had fathered eleven sons and a daughter, Jacob asked Laban to allow him to return to Canaan, his home, but Laban asked him to stay since Jacob's industriousness had made Laban a very rich man. The two struck a bargain that Jacob was able to use to greatly enrich himself as well. Laban and his sons became angry and, this time at the Lord's behest, Jacob fled, taking his wives and flocks as well as Laban's idols, which Rachel had taken without Jacob's knowledge.

At one point during his journey, Jacob wrestled through the night with "a Man" (Gen. 32:24) variously interpreted to be an actual man, an angel, a Christophany (or preincarnational appearance of Christ), or God the Father. Whichever it was, Jacob asked afterward for a blessing, and his opponent complied, saying, "Your name shall no longer be called Jacob, but Israel; for you have struggled with God and with men, and have prevailed" (v. 28).

The name *Israel* means "he who struggles with God" or

even "having power with God." Jacob's new identity made it clear that his mission and his power came from his relationship with God, not from his own power or machinations, and the nation that took Israel's name can be found throughout the Old Testament responding to God with questions and challenges as well as with love and submission.

Back to Bethel

In Genesis 35, God called Jacob back to the place of that first blessing, to that place where God was fresh and alive within him, where he had been excited enough about God to make his vow. God is calling you back to that very place as well. That is the true nature of reset. For most of us, that place is just as special, just as memorable as it was for Jacob. After all, that is the place where the Lord and his grace found us. When you got saved and started on your journey of faith, you no doubt had a marvelous honeymoon experience. But then, life happened. You began to drift. You began to focus more attention elsewhere. It's not that you didn't love God. It's just that you got busy at school. You got busy with work. You got busy with the cares of the world. You no longer prayed like you once did. You didn't read God's Word like you once did. You didn't take the things of God as seriously as you once did.

Fortunately, the God we serve is the God of the second chance. He authorizes spiritual U-turns. Ours is a God who loves you in spite of the path you've taken. No matter what you've done, no matter how far off you've wandered, you are a candidate for a reset.

It was sin that drove Jacob from his peace, from everything that was normal in his life. That is what sin does. His own misdeeds forced him to flee from his brother, Esau. Sin will always have you on the run. I see so many people whose actions have stripped them of peace and normalcy. When Adam and Eve sinned, they were driven out of the Garden of Eden. When Peter sinned and denied the Lord, he "went out and wept bitterly" (Matt. 26:75).

Fortunately, the God we serve is the God of the second chance.

It may have been sin that drove Jacob to Bethel—the name means "house of God"—but when he found God there, everything changed. The Lord met him in the midst of his mess. That in itself made Bethel a place of great victory.

Our messes do not disqualify us. They do not stop God from meeting us right in the middle of them. That is one of the glorious realities of God's nature and of our relationship with him. We can be running from God, we can be doing our own thing, but God finds us right where we are. "Those who are well have no need of a physician," said Jesus. "I did not come to call the righteous, but sinners" (Mark 2:17).

As he spoke to Jacob, God will speak to you, and when God speaks, he has already factored in where you are in your life. He is aware of your situation. He is aware of your destiny. And it's important to note that God does not give suggestions. God gives commands. God's call to Jacob in Genesis 35:1 was a command to go back to the place where he started. "Arise, go up to Bethel and dwell there; and make an altar there to God." He wanted Jacob back in the place where God had found him. And that is where God wants you.

Back Where He Found You

As he calls us to reset, God is saying to each of us, "I want you back in the place where I found you." For Jacob, it was a physical place, the place where that incredible dream caused him to wake up knowing something had changed and that he was ready to meet the Lord's promises with promises of his own.

Too many of us have gotten so far away from that place where our worship was sincere and our excitement was palpable that we don't understand what it means to go back. But we can take consolation in knowing that Jacob was in a similar place. By chapter 35, it had been twenty years since his flight from Esau and that moment when God found him. Jacob had drifted, as we often do. He had been inundated with carnality, and he found himself intermingled with idols. He had gone cold against God. He was no longer the worshiper that he was in chapter 28.

That's what happens to us when we get caught up in the world. We come to church and think God is impressed by our praise, but there is a distinct difference between praise and worship. Praise is simply a response to what God has done for us. You don't have to know God deeply or be mature in your faith to praise God, and praise often gets intermingled with a spirit of entitlement among church people. "As long as God is my heavenly bail man and does what I ask him to do, I will praise him," is how we look at it. "I will praise God for my house. I will praise God for my car. I will praise God for my scholarship or my sweet boo."

I see that sort of mind-set all the time. I will know what your relationship with God is if you lose your house, if you lose your car, if you lose your scholarship, if you lose your boo. If your relationship is real, you won't sit there with your lip stuck out. You won't take a sabbatical from church. You will come in to the house of God and you will declare, "I will still worship God. I will still give God glory because the Lord gave and the Lord has taken away. Blessed be the name of the Lord."

God was telling Jacob to go back to that place where his relationship with God was authentic, where his worship was sincere, and each of us is Jacob when it is time to reset. Think about where the Lord found you. Think about your Bethel. Think about when the Lord saved you and what he saved you from. Think about the grace he so freely offered. Remember where you were, what you were caught up in, how tangled up your life was. Think about the bad choices you made. And yet God saved you.

Commitment and Promise

Let's look more closely at that meeting as Jacob experienced it. This was a place of spiritual commitment, and God made promises to Jacob:

- He promised him land.
- He promised him blessing.
- He promised him protection.
- He promised him provision.
- He promised him his presence.

And Jacob made a threefold promise of his own:

- You will be my Lord wherever I go.
- I will set up this stone as a memorial because I want people to know where you met me.
- Whatever you bless me with, I will give a tenth back to you.

To take on that first promise of Jacob is to recognize God in every aspect of our lives. We are no longer just Sunday Christians. We become his people, and others can see the light that shines within us, day in and day out.

To take on the second is to acknowledge that it is God's presence in our lives that has changed us. It is to recognize that God has found us and lifted us from where we were. It is to be unafraid to share that part of our story when it will bring hope to others.

To take on the third promise is to make sure we give back to God in all things. Any relationship with God is reciprocal, and we are to share our material as well as our spiritual blessings. Jacob's third promise is also an indication that the tithe was established well before God gave Moses the Law. There are those who say that tithing is of the old covenant. This shows us that it was pre-Mosaic covenant.

> We become his people, and others can see the light that shines within us, day in and day out.

So many of us have spiritual amnesia. We act like the Lord didn't find us in a place of sin, out of control, in a downward spiral. When you remember where God found you, you begin to realize that God deserves so much more than you are giving him right now—so much more praise, so much more time, so much more glory. When you think about how far God has brought you, it will make you want to return to that place where your appreciation was fresh. It will make you look at your shortcomings and say, "I've got to get my life together. I've got to go back to God. I'm ready to return to the way things used to be."

Does your life look like this?

- Are you just praising God in church or not at all?
- Are you so lost in the music on your car stereo that you haven't prayed in your car in months or years?
- Are you so busy that prayer has to wait until this show goes off and that show goes off and maybe just

one more and before long you're too tired to pray at all or you fall asleep while you're praying?

- Is your Bible just something that lies on the table until Sunday morning, when you grab it to take it to church? Do you pick it up at all?

Return to Me

We need to be like the prodigal son who came back to his senses and said, "I will go back to my father's house, even if I have to be a servant. I've got to go back to the place where I know I need to be" (Luke 15:17–19, author's paraphrase).

In Malachi 3:7, God says, "Return to Me, and I will return to you." But the return he asks for is a complete one. And so I must ask you:

- Do you remember exactly where that place was?
- Do you remember when you would praise God just by yourself?
- Do you remember when you would be in your car, tears running down your face, and you were giving God glory, and you would forget the light had turned green?
- Do you remember when your Bible was full of highlighted text, with notes in the margins, and you were like a sponge soaking up God's Word?

- Do you remember getting lost in prayer in the evening, looking for guidance, praising his name, taking the good and bad of your day to him?
- Do you remember the time when nobody had to beg you to come to church and you would be in the house of God often, giving God glory?
- Do you remember when you weren't too tired or when it didn't matter how much rain was coming down, and you would give God glory?
- Do you remember the time when you thought about the goodness of Jesus and all he did for you and you couldn't help but praise him?

That's where God is trying to get you back to! "Jacob, arise, go to Bethel. Settle there" (Gen. 35:1, author's paraphrase). God is saying, "You are living too low. The places you dwell, the people you associate with, the standards you set are all too low. You are too anointed to be where you are."

The only sensible response is, "I'm getting away from low-down people. I'm tired of people who don't want anything and don't want anybody else to have anything. Lord, lift me up. Let me stand. Plant my feet on higher ground."

Can you come back to that place?

Can you come back to first things?

Can you reset your worship?

Can you recommit yourself to do the things you did before you drifted so far away?

God Is Speaking to Us

We are all Jacobs, and though it may be twenty years since we've been on fire, God never stops seeking us. No matter how far we drift, God keeps talking to us. In fact, sometimes when you're doing your dirt, you really wish God would just be silent. But God keeps reminding you, keeps saying, "I'm still talking to you." You may be out there twerking and dropping it like it's hot, but you know you still hear God's voice because after you get in your car and turn on the radio, there's God talking. Driving down the street, you see a billboard, and there's God talking. Somebody walks by you with a T-shirt on, and there's God talking. You see a member of the church—there's God talking. Everywhere you look, every time you turn around, God is talking to you. You try to hide your Bible, you put away your religious CDs, but there's God, still talking.

When Adam and Eve sinned, the voice of God went walking in the garden looking for them. I don't care what situation you find yourself in, God is talking to you right now. You are not reading this book by accident. God is right here with you, saying, "Get up out of the low place. Pull your life back together. Reset. Get back to Bethel. Go back to the place where I first called you."

> No matter how far we drift, God keeps talking to us.

Just do what 1 John 1:9 says: "If we confess our sins, He is faithful and just to forgive us our sins and to cleanse us from all unrighteousness."

Come back to that place where you and God first exchanged vows and find yourself reinvigorated. But get ready because when you do, you can expect big things to happen.

Isaiah Calls the People of Israel to Reset Again

"Come now, and let us reason together,"
Says the Lord,
"Though your sins are like scarlet,
They shall be as white as snow;
Though they are red like crimson,
They shall be as wool."
—Isaiah 1:18

One of Scripture's recurring themes is God's call to his people to turn back to him, and one of the most dramatic examples comes in the opening chapter of Isaiah. This passage is often referred to as the prophet's first published sermon. Many theologians, including John Calvin, believed that the custom of the prophets was to hang a copy of their sermon on the temple doorpost, that those who would enter might see and hear what God was saying to them firsthand.

Whether you consider it in its written form or imagine Isaiah himself preaching it, this is a powerful sermon leveling five charges against the people of God:

- They were not representing the Jewish nation as they should. They were hypocritical.
- They had a spirit of ingratitude. God had done so much for them, but in their narcissism they acted as though they had done these things themselves.
- They were so corrupted that God could not bring reform to the nation, reform he desired to bring about if only the people would turn from their wickedness.
- Universal corruption was everywhere you looked. Their systems and inner workings had degenerated.
- Their rulers were perverse. Those expected to set the example were among the worst offenders.

Whenever we see God's people admonished in Scripture, it is worth our while to see ourselves in their actions, and it's plain to see that we are much like the people of Israel. The good news is that we also share with them the opportunity to live inside God's solutions, for, finally, after listing their transgressions, telling them, "Your hands are full of blood," and promising death as the price of continued disobedience, God offered an olive branch. In verse 18, he reached out with an earnest call to repentance and reformation. He offered life if they would just learn to do good—in other words, if they would reset.

We also share with them the opportunity to live inside God's solutions.

"Let us reason together," says Isaiah. This is God calling them and us—not tomorrow, not six months down the road, but now. This is a call for immediate action.

The Lord pleads often with us to choose his way. "I call heaven and earth to witness against you this day," says Deuteronomy 30:19 (RSV), "that I have set before you life and death, blessing and curse; therefore choose life, that you and your descendants may live."

Timing

Most of us don't get the sudden blinding light Saul did. We don't have our transgressions posted on the church door. We often procrastinate when it comes to the choice to reset, in large part because it means giving up the things that keep us from God. We are drawn to those things, and many of us won't turn away from them until they've brought us trouble and turmoil, until we've experienced the chaos and destruction that accompany our vices.

Reset requires the willingness to declare, "Lord, I'm done. I'm going to reel some things in." It requires stepping up. Paul said, "When I was a child, I spoke like a child, I thought like a child, I reasoned like a child. When I became a man, I gave up childish ways" (1 Cor. 13:11 ESV). The difference is what stepping into that reset moment can accomplish.

God is a God of timing. He operates in *kairos* rather than *chronos*—his time, not ours. He knows exactly where to meet us because he knows our journeys in their entirety, and he knows how to get our undivided attention. There comes a moment for each of us when that happens, when we realize *now is the time.* And until you realize that, you will remain in that messed-up situation, you will stay on the street, doing your dirt, outside of God's will.

It's time.

This is not about time on the clock. In this case, God's *kairos* moment is when you recognize that something in your spirit is saying, "I am tired. I am fed up. I need a change." It is the moment when God sends you the word. He too is saying, "I am fed up. I have had enough of your perverse proclivities. I have had enough of your dirty dealings. I have had enough of your sanctimonious sacrifices. I am tired, weary of seeing you in a position of being sick and tired because of your own sin and corruption." He is requesting an audience, one-on-one, with an offer that can resolve your situation, no matter how corrupt and chaotic.

And when God says it's time, it's time. Ask Saul. Ask Ananias. Ask Jonah.

"Let us reason together," says Isaiah 1:18. Let us talk this through. Let us argue it out.

There are huge consequences to this call. Without that choice to reset, there is death. The call to reset is God's calling us on the carpet, saying, "I'm going to deal with you straight-up"—something he will do both when he is blessing us and when he is confronting us. God wants us to be just as straight-up—and there's no point in trying to hide, since he knows us, our situations, and our proclivities anyway!

This is God urging us to break through our wall of separation. There is distance between our will and God's will. There is a gulf between what we want and what God wants. There is a paradigm shift between rebellion and obedience. And there is a fundamental difference between feeling bad about a situation and truly being convicted about it. You can feel bad about being pulled over for speeding. You can look sorrowful enough that the police officer says, "All right. I'm just giving you a warning, but slow down from now on."

"Yes, Officer, I'll do that," you say, but you're hardly out of sight before you're speeding again. Remorse is not conviction.

The only thing big enough to bridge that gap between our will and God's is reset—a fundamental, hard reset.

It's when you get weary enough of doing it your way that you'll really surrender, and the gateway to deliverance is often just that—being tired enough to see the light and hear the voice.

There is nothing wrong with being tired, if you're tired of being played, tired of a dysfunctional relationship, tired of trifling friends, tired of being up all night, tired of hangovers, tired of playing games. In fact, often God cannot get your attention if you're not tired, played out, spent down to your marrow. If you're still doing what you're doing and caught up in it, God says, "I can't work with you. I can only work with folks who are out of strength and out of fight."

Stop Struggling

There was a young boy trying to show off for the young girls at the beach. He jumped on his surfboard and paddled out to where the big waves were. He looked cocky and confident, but the reality was that underneath his swagger, he couldn't swim. As he tried to ride those waves, he suddenly realized they were much bigger and stronger than he was. Soon he was overtaken, knocked from that board into the ocean. This was much more than he had bargained for. In an instant he was scrambling for his life, trying with real desperation to turn his thrashing about into real swimming. He and the people on the shore both realized rather quickly that his efforts weren't going to be enough.

Among those onlookers was a lifeguard, a tanned, muscular young man who looked calm and collected behind his reflective shades. You would have thought he would spring into action and sprint toward the water to rescue our young show-off, but the lifeguard just sat there looking. The boy went down once and came back up.

"Heeelllllp!" he yelled, struggling as only the truly scared can struggle. "I can't swim!"

The lifeguard slowly took off his shades and leaned forward to look more closely at him. The boy went down and bobbed up again.

"Heeelllllp!" he yelled, with even more panic in his voice. "Please help."

With a little more animation, the lifeguard climbed down off his perch and walked to the edge of the water.

The boy went down again, and came up a little more slowly this time. His cry for help was a shadow of what it once was. He was no longer struggling. Quickly the lifeguard swam out to him, placed one arm under his, and swam with him back to the shore. There he let the boy cough and sputter until the water was out of his lungs. The boy panted, wild-eyed, until he finally caught his breath. When he had regained his senses and his strength and had pulled the seaweed from his face, he turned with real anger toward the lifeguard.

"What's wrong with you? What kind of lifeguard are you? I almost drowned out there!"

"A pretty good one, actually," said the lifeguard.

"What do you mean by that?" said the boy. "Another minute and I'd have died!"

"Well," said the lifeguard, "if I had gone straight out to you while you were thrashing around as hard as you were, you would have taken me under with you. I had to wait until you were too tired to struggle before I could safely rescue you."

You may be one of those people to whom God is saying, "I'm going to let you keep on struggling. I am going to wait right here until you say, 'Lord, I'm tired. I resign. I'm done.'"

It's at that point that God will step in—or swim out—and rescue you. That is when he can change your circumstance.

Just because he is waiting doesn't mean God doesn't have the power or the will to save you. On the contrary, there is no circumstance, no depth of sin, no manner of human condition that he can't overturn. No matter what you've been caught up in, God is sufficient. He has the power to change you.

He just needs you to stop struggling.

REFLECTIONS

- Have you been the beneficiary of God's promises?
- What promises have you made God in return? Have you kept them?
- Have you discerned God's plan for your life? Where would you start?
- Do you feel as though you have moved away from that plan?
- Is your current choice of friends and circumstances shortchanging your position as a child of God?
- Are you prepared for God to meet you where you are? Are there other people who might act as guides to help you?

CHAPTER 5

RECLAIM AND REDEDICATE

Once we have decided to heed the call to reset, what must we do? In order to get back to that place where everything was fresh, we must go through a process of purification. Jacob knew that truth. Sin had taken hold where he resided, so purification had to take place.

Sometimes we have to distance ourselves physically from things, the activities and the people, that have hindered us from a relationship with God. Sometimes more than a physical distance is required—there must be a separation from the proclivities and mind-sets that keep us from God.

There can be no purification without separation, and there can be no separation without some agitation. Sin has attached itself to you the way dirt and grime attach themselves to your clothes. To remove it, there has to be agitation. In real life that can mean disruption. There are relationships you've been in where you've been calling people, wondering, *Why don't they call me back? What did I do?* God is saying, "You didn't do anything. I am purposely agitating this thing, removing you from the people and things that bring down your value so I might take you to where you're supposed to be."

Thank God for that kind of agitation. That is God telling you to stop stalking people he has released from your life: Quit stalking them on Facebook and Twitter. Utilize the delete button on your phone. Stop being so loyal to losers. Stop being so committed to carnality. Stop being so focused on foolishness.

Jacob and his family members had to let their deities go. They had idols, false gods among them, and since those were among the things that stood in their way, they had to remove them all.

What about you? Where are your idols? Whatever takes your time, money, or devotion away from God has become your God. Those things clothe you in filthy garments. God says, "I need you to remove the idols. I need you to cleanse yourself of their dirtiness."

We gradually take on the attributes of the people and places we are mixed up with. We begin to look like them and behave like them, and to those who view us, we are indistinguishable from them. They become the things that define and defile us. God says, "It's time for you to change your garments." The psalmist, after he had recognized just how defiled he had become, said in Psalm 51:7, "Purge me with hyssop, and I shall be clean; wash me, and I shall be whiter than snow."

Reset involves creating distance between you and what was. Jacob told his wives and his entourage, "You are going back to Bethel with me. Give me all the gold out of your ears and everything that relates to idols." Jacob took all of that and hid it under the terebinth tree near Shechem—in other words, he buried it. That's an important moment because there are things we need to bury too. The trouble is, too many of us bury things like a dog buries them, shallowly, only to come back to them later on a rainy day. You might say, "I'm done with him. It's over. I bury this relationship." Then your options run out, and you're feeling lonely, and the next thing you know you're digging him back up again.

If you are going to bury it, bury it! Hold a funeral and walk away. Move on. Ashes to ashes and dust to dust. Jacob did just that, burying those things in Shechem, then moving on, because his destiny was in Bethel.

> Reset involves creating distance between you and what was.

How Long Will You Linger?

But what about you? How long will you linger between Shechem and Bethel? How long will you tiptoe back, unable to leave Shechem behind for good? Say good-bye, and move on, once and for all, to Bethel.

The positive consequences of doing so are there for us to see in Jacob's story. Once he had buried the past and moved on, he was given protection. "And they journeyed, and the terror of God was upon the cities that were all around them," says Genesis 35:5, "and they did not pursue the sons of Jacob."

Jacob had done it right. He buried his past, took his family, and went to Bethel, where it had all started and where he had been called. As the text makes clear, he still faced enemies, as we might, when we leave the past behind. You letting the devil go doesn't mean the devil is going to let you go. But the Bible says God will send out a heavenly memo and let every hater know, "Don't you touch my children because I fight their battles."

When you do what God tells you to do, God will often block attacks. In fact, you may not even know about it, as he often fights battles behind the scenes. "No weapon formed against you shall prosper," says Isaiah 54:17. He's got you covered.

Once you have made your way back to Bethel, get ready to reconnect with God. This is what God has wanted all along: for you to experience *true* connection with him.

Many years ago my refrigerator suddenly stopped working. When I looked behind it, I determined that it was plugged in. That was the extent of my knowledge of refrigerator mechanics. Since it was over my head, I called a repair service. There was a service charge the moment the man walked in the door, but he knew more than I did, so even though money was hard to come by at that point, I was glad to pay it. The tech started by taking a look behind the refrigerator at the plug.

"I've already done that," I said, maybe a little too self-assuredly. He took the flashlight from his tool belt and shone it on that plug. Then he reached down and just eased it in about half an inch. At that moment the power came back on. Believe me when I tell you it had seemed connected to me. I just didn't have an experienced eye.

Some of us look like we're plugged in, but we're not. We're just half an inch or so from the power source. You might shout, but you can't cast out demons. You might run, but you're still depressed. You might jump up, but the devil has taken over your family. I am here to tell you that God wants you to have full power. God wants you to have complete connection. He wants you to plug back in, and when you plug in, you once again have what you've been missing.

The problem of being disconnected from God can be dramatic. Your life is filled with chaos and has become one drama after another. Nothing you've been trying to accomplish is working out. You can't seem to make anything happen. Your career, your relationships, seem stalled or worse. You're giving your all and—nothing.

"What's going on? Why can't I sleep at night? Why can't I get in a healthy relationship?"

"What's going on, pastor? My money's a mess. Why am I going through this?"

It's because you've lost your connection with God, and

God is not the author of confusion. God is the author of peace. that's an invitation to confusion. God is not the author of confusion. God is the author of peace. Reconnecting, resetting, will reorient your priorities. He says, "When you connect with me, you'll discover it's not about the stuff that money can buy. It's about the stuff money can't buy."

Build Your Altar

Then, like Jacob, you must build your altar. What does that look like? An altar is meant for sacrifice. In this case the altar is a symbol of your willingness to sacrifice. That is something we have too often lost sight of here in America. We have been spoiled. We have creature comforts. We have food in our refrigerators. We have cushioned pews in air-conditioned churches. We have nice cars and buildings with climate controls. Many of us have garages so that when it's raining, we just pull in and walk into our homes and offices without getting wet.

Want a lesson in renewal? Look no further than our brothers and sisters in Africa. They don't have easy access to food. They don't have air-conditioning. They don't have cars, much less climate-controlled ones. Still, they fill places of worship every Sunday morning. Some of them are getting up at 4:00 a.m. and walking five or even ten miles on blistered feet to sit with lizards and scorpions, sometimes in tents, sometimes in stadiums, to worship. They're not wondering what they'll be doing come Sunday. They're not worried about the weather. They fill places of worship, and they are wide-eyed and happy to be there. They are praising God and giving him the glory. Their worship is pure and so holy. And we have to be begged to come to church in our big, air-conditioned cars, and too often we sit with our arms folded as the preacher preaches. We have much to learn about the concept of sacrifice.

> The altar is a symbol of your willingness to sacrifice.

In the days of Jesus the temple was for offering sacrifices for atonement. Animals died on the altar. If you want to regroup, if you're ready to reset, something within you has to die that you might live like you have never lived before. When you build your altar, your past has to die, your self-entitlement has to die, your me-first attitude has to die. Just as you don't want to dig up what you've buried of your past, don't bring something to the altar and then take it back the next week.

God says, "There are some things I need you to let die so you can experience the joy of the Lord." This is your invitation. God has been telling you to regroup. You're not praying like you were praying. Perhaps your Bible is open only on Sundays now, and you're praying only over your food. God is saying, *regroup.*

If you want your fire back, if you want to experience the passion of a new believer again, something within you must die. What relationship, what addiction, is holding you back? What is hindering you from regaining your place in God today?

If you're ready to build your altar, you can't worry about what others will think. You can't be concerned with who does or doesn't like you and who does or doesn't want to be around you. And you have to realize that no one else can build your altar for you.

If you want your fire back, if you want to experience the passion of a new believer again, something within you must die.

If you have heard God's voice saying, "It's time to get back to Bethel," then begin the process. Leave Shechem, return to Bethel, and build the altar to the one who found you in your mess.

Conviction and Choice

"I have given you a land for which you did not labor, and cities which you did not build, and you dwell in them; you eat of the vineyards and olive groves which you did not plant. Now therefore, fear the LORD, serve Him in sincerity and in truth, and put away the gods which your fathers served on the other side of the River and in Egypt. Serve the LORD! And if it seems evil to you to serve the LORD, choose for yourselves this day whom you will serve, whether the gods which your fathers served that were on the other side of the River, or the gods of the Amorites, in whose land you dwell. But as for me and my house, we will serve the LORD."

—JOSHUA 24:13–15

Many people live between two realities. On the one hand, they want to be spiritual. They want to receive blessings from the Lord and walk on his path. On the other hand, they can't let go of the world. This world has pleasures they mistake for blessings, and it's hard for some people to choose. Some, in fact, are content with living between those two realities, and others simply haven't made clear where they stand with regard to the things of the Lord.

God expects conviction. He expects us to be on fire for the things of the Lord. Revelation 3:16 says that if you are lukewarm, "I will spue thee out of my mouth" (KJV).

Still, it's worth making clear that God also wants us to have balance. It is possible to carry anything, even our expressions of commitment to the things of God, too far. Nobody wants to hear someone they've invited over to watch the big game prophesying over your life five minutes in. There is a difference between spiritual living and spiritual buffoonery.

> God expects conviction. He expects us to be on fire for the things of the Lord.

But now, just as in the days of Joshua, God is looking for commitment, for people who are serious about stepping up and living out his truth, and so it's important that we learn the lessons of those days. Israel had come into the promised land. Her enemies had been vanquished. Each of the tribes of Israel had received its inheritance. It was a time of peace and prosperity, of hope and blessing. The promise had come to fruition.

But the people of God must have been aware that in the midst of their comfort, they had allowed themselves to become self-satisfied. They had been lulled by their very prosperity, by the goodness of the Lord upon their lives. They had intermingled with the gods of the Canaanites. The idolatry around them had infiltrated their hearts.

All of us have to be mindful that we can drift into such states as well. None of us is beyond letting our guard down. The moment you walk into a place where the promises of God have been made manifest, it is easy to find yourself slipping. Before long you find yourself enmeshed with the cares of the world.

So many people, as long as the job keeps paying, as long as their health is good, as long as everything is going well, are content. In America, if there is no natural disaster, if there is no terrorist attack, there is less inclination to think about God. But the moment we meet tragedy, everybody wants to come together. We call prayer meetings at the Capitol. The news channels bring on the preachers, asking, "What is God saying?"

You need to know that in times of ease, in times of plenty, you had better have your relationship with God right. You might want to question the authenticity of that relationship if you only go to him when you're in trouble. Joshua understood this completely. He literally stood up and challenged the people of God, telling them that God demands full allegiance, full investment. God wants us to live completely for him.

Solemn Assembly

Joshua did this in the course of a solemn assembly, in which he gathered the people and leaders of all the tribes of Israel. It was a momentous event.

Any time the people of God come together, you witness collective power, an undeniable synergy. Hebrews 10:25 urges us not to forsake "the assembling of ourselves together." One of the great examples took place in Acts 2 on the Day of Pentecost, when the people came together "with one accord" (v. 1), and power came down and filled them.

Things begin to happen when the people of God gather. "Where two or three are gathered together in my name," Jesus said in Matthew 18:20, "there am I in the midst" (KJV). Something powerful takes place when we are together and the power of God is among us.

Joshua called the people together and reminded them of the power and wonder of their history. "God has redeemed you," he told them. He then reminded them of the foundational event of their history, when the entire nation of Israel

Something powerful takes place when we are together and the power of God is among us. was reset, saying, "God has delivered you out of the land of Egypt!" He took them through the Exodus to the settling of the promised land, telling them how God had manifested his power and glory on their behalf time and time again. He reminded them of the victories they had achieved. He wanted them to realize—to feel down to their marrow—how far God had brought them.

Look over your own life and recall where you were when the Lord found you. This is something you may be reluctant to discuss because you don't want people to realize just how messed up your life was at one point. Like so many people, you want others to think you've always been well-dressed, that you've always been in control, that you have always had it going on.

But there is power in the testimony of those who will talk about where they've come from. If you knew where the Lord found many of us, you would understand why we run like we run, why we shout like we shout, why we are so certain that the power of God has been at work in our lives. Only God's power can change lives the way ours have been changed. Only God's power is able to turn a life around the way your life was turned—or the way it needs to be turned. Week in and week out I see the power of God all over my church. Joshua saw it stretched out in front of him as he called the people together. His job was to help them see it, the way mine is to help you see it.

The Necessity of Sacrifice

Joshua was saying to them, "Understand this very clearly, Israel, that without the presence of God, you would never have the covenant of God, but without sacrifice, God's presence would mean nothing for you. Understand that God has always been among you, but God only admits or allows his presence where there is sacrifice."

Every successful athlete knows the importance of sacrifice. There is first the reality that to be in top condition, you have to dedicate a great deal of time to training. Those who don't use the off-season for conditioning are at a severe disadvantage when the next season's training camp opens. Then there is the study of playbooks and a great deal of practice, running plays, and getting a feel for game conditions. Finally, there is the fact that since a team is a unit, individual egos and accolades must be secondary to team accomplishment and unity.

Everyone in a successful marriage knows the importance of sacrifice. A me-first attitude in a marriage is a recipe for disaster. Marriage is a partnership best nurtured with giving and selflessness.

And every successful Christian must know the importance of sacrifice. We are called to feed the hungry, clothe the naked, visit the sick and imprisoned. In other words, we are called to give of ourselves, to "love your neighbor as yourself" (Mark 12:31). We all know what this looks like: you tithe, give money to worthy projects, and spend your Saturdays cleaning up the local playground, delivering meals, or visiting someone in an assisted living or nursing home. There are so many ways in which our time and our money can make a difference. Done in a spirit of selflessness, you quickly find that something that might seem onerous at first becomes pure joy, an expression of the spirit working through us. Loving God by helping others is an ideal way to manifest God's presence in the world.

Every successful Christian must know the importance of sacrifice.

In all areas of life the benefits of sacrifice far outweigh the price of anything we might have given up. Self-sacrifice in athletics leads to success on the field. Within marriage, it leads to harmony. And on the spiritual front, it leads to the kind of riches only God can provide.

Those riches were on Joshua's mind, particularly in the way the people had benefitted from the faithfulness of their ancestors Abraham, Isaac, and Jacob. Joshua called the people to understand God's power, his presence, and his provision. They were in the place they had dreamed of, and he reminded them of the words of Deuteronomy 6:10–12:

> "So it shall be, when the LORD your God brings you into the land of which He swore to your fathers, to Abraham, Isaac, and Jacob, to give you large and beautiful cities which you did not build, houses full of all good things, which you did not fill, hewn-out wells which you did not

dig, vineyards and olive trees which you did not plant—when you have eaten and are full—then beware, lest you forget the LORD who brought you out of the land of Egypt, from the house of bondage."

This was the promised land, and Joshua had to remind the people to view it as such and to be grateful. Abraham's ticket to God's blessings was obedience. Here, God was asking, first and foremost, that Abraham's descendants simply not have amnesia. God led the people of Israel to the promised land and did everything he said he was going to do. Joshua was there to remind the people not to act like they had done it themselves. "God provided for you and has protected you," he said. "Look at all that God has done. You're alive, in Canaan, with things you don't deserve, safe from your enemies. Just don't act like you did it yourselves. Recognize the source!"

The True Source

It's the same with us. What can you say you have earned with your goodness or dedication to the Lord? What do you really deserve when it's all tallied? Can you in good conscience sit in church with your arms folded and act like you did it all yourself?

As Joshua called the people to rededicate themselves in light of God's blessings, we are called to be mindful of the favors of God that have echoed through the ages and redounded to our benefit. God has been present in our own darkest times. He is there when you are in the valley of the shadow of death. He is there when friends and family forsake you. The notion that Israel's success was its own doing or that your life is your own doing is foolish. What I have, God gave me. What I am, God made me. Where I am, God brought me. What I know, God taught me.

In both cases—Israel's and ours—God knows exactly when to confront those who have wandered off, who have let their attention drift from his central role as the source of our blessings. In verse 14 of chapter 24, Joshua says, "Now therefore, fear the LORD, serve Him in sincerity and in truth, and put away the gods which your fathers served on the other side of the River and in Egypt. Serve the LORD!"

> [God] is there when friends and family forsake you.

"That is not the way we are to conduct ourselves here," he is saying. "This is not Egypt."

"Fear the Lord" means, of course, to view God with the reverence he deserves, to acknowledge the awe he inspires. "Before you left Egypt, you had a reverence for God," he tells them. "Now that you're prospering outside of Egypt, you don't."

It's that way with so many today. When everything's good, when there's no crisis, reverence for God wanes. People change his Word to suit themselves. They desecrate God's holy places with evil intentions. They blaspheme God's name. They put a cross on their necks while they're dropping it like it's hot. They come to church lit. They lust even among the people of God.

There used to be a time when even the wino walking down the street would cross the street and take off his hat when he was about to pass the church because he had a reverence for God. The fear of the Lord is the beginning of knowledge, and few have that fear the way people used to have it.

"Put away your gods," says Joshua. Put away the things that lie between you and God. Put your toys up. When you were a child, you thought as a child, you understood as a child, but you're grown now. Put away those gods. Serve the Lord with sincerity.

The Real Thing

The word *sincere*, interestingly enough, comes from Latin words meaning "without wax." It stems from the days when potters would make expensive pottery, but if the pots cracked during the process, they filled the cracks with wax, then painted over them. That way no one could tell there was a deformity—unless they put something hot into the pottery. Then the heat would melt the wax, and the pottery might break apart. But when Jeremiah saw the potter working at the wheel in Jeremiah 18, he saw that this potter didn't put wax on marred pots. He shattered them and started over. He did not take that which was cracked and try to make allowances for it or hide its imperfections.

Smart buyers knew if they held a piece of pottery up to the sunlight, they would be able to see the flaws under the paint. God says there are a lot of people living in such a way that you can't tell they're not the real thing. They praise, they lift their hands in worship, they run, they sing, they make a lot of noise in church, but if you hold them up to the light, you'll find they're full of wax.

It's up to us to make up our minds and say, "Lord, I want to be the real thing! I don't want to be touched up with wax. I want to serve you sincerely. Let whatever is in my life be real." The question is, are your priorities in order? Joshua 24:15 says, "And if it seems evil to you to serve the LORD, choose for yourselves this day whom you will serve, whether the gods which your fathers served that were on the other side of the River, or the gods of the Amorites, in whose land you dwell."

And who or what are you going to serve? Are you going to serve your car? Are you going to worship your job or your career? Are you going to serve the love of your life? Are you going to worship your jewelry? Now is the time to choose. But remember, whatever you choose today to worship, when you get in trouble, turn to that. If you choose your car, when you're in trouble, go to your car and say, "Help me!" When you're sick, turn to your job. When you're down and out, run to your jewelry for comfort. When your money dries up, go to your boo and see what happens.

"Lord, I want to be the real thing!"

You know and I know what you can expect if you do that. We both know where your help comes from. Matthew 6:24

says, "No one can serve two masters; for either he will hate the one and love the other, or else he will be loyal to the one and despise the other. You cannot serve God and mammon."

As for Me and My House

Joshua offers himself as a paradigm. "But as for me and my house," he says to the multitude, "we will serve the LORD" (24:15).

We are responsible for ourselves and our households. I don't have time to be in your business. I have plenty to deal with in mine. Like Joshua, each of us needs to develop backbone and declare plainly, "Me and my house will serve the Lord."

Instead, we have far too many wishy-washy saints. We don't know where they stand from one day to the next. We need saints who will say, "Lord, I want to be what you want me to be." Too many of us are mercurial. We are easily cowed, easily swayed. The opinions of others can move us into or away from almost anything. You and I are not here for those people. We need to reach the point where we declare, "I'll let nothing separate me from the Lord."

It is time for consecration. Look carefully at verses 16–17:

So the people answered and said: "Far be it from us that we should forsake the LORD to serve other gods; for the LORD our God is He who brought us and our fathers up out of the land of Egypt, from the house of bondage, who did those great signs in our sight, and preserved us in all the way that we went and among all the people through whom we passed."

In other words, "Since you put it that way, Joshua, we have come to our senses! We remember that God did all this!"

Everything I have is on loan from the Lord. It isn't my house. It isn't my car. It isn't my money. No one but God did it. I would be delusional if I did not serve a God like that.

My question to you today is, if you had a list of priorities, where would God be on that list? And if God has to compete for your time and attention, your love or your money, then is God really your first priority?

Two Realities

Let's juxtapose two things for a moment. Let's look at how faithful you are to two opposing realities—God and your boo, meaning the boo you had, the boo you have, or the boo you want. Let's see how faithful you are.

For your boo, nothing is too expensive. You would go into debt to impress your boo. "I want the best one you have," you tell the clerk in the jewelry store. "This is for somebody special." You'll save up for your boo. When it comes to God, though, "That's just too much money to be giving to the church."

For your boo, no weather is too bad to call off a visit.

There can be a tornado watch, you might have to walk through the mud with your umbrella to get to the car, you may get soaked walking to his or her door, but you'll do what you have to, just to get close. When it comes to God, the sky can just hint at rain, and you'll say, "I think I'm going to stay home and just stream the service," when streaming is actually meant for folks who are unable to get to the church and for those who are out of town, not for the locals.

For your boo, no distance is too great. You'll drive all the way across town, you'll go to every mall in the county, looking to find just the right thing, but when it comes to God, well, every mile counts with gas prices the way they are.

For your boo, there's no such thing as "It's too late," or "It's too early." You'll get up at one in the morning when you get that call, and you'll get dressed and be there within the hour. But for God, you can't stay alert even through a ninety-minute service. You leave before the benediction. You're just too tired to sit through it all.

For your boo, no sacrifice is too great. You'll carve out time, take a vacation day, take off work, do whatever you have to do to be with your boo, but for God, "I'm busy. I've got too much to do. I'm working overtime."

When it comes to your boo, your joys are written on your face. We can tell when you're boo'd up because you have that glow and pep in your step. Every time we see you, you're smiling and happy, but for God, you sit in church looking as though you're sucking on lemons, like you've been tore up from the floor up.

You have to make up your mind that God is the best thing that's ever happened to you. Get excited! Get over the top! Radiate the truth that God has been too good to you. When you praise God, let people know. Tell somebody, "I searched all over and couldn't find anybody greater than him. I've made up my mind that I'm on the Lord's side."

So what about you? Are you going to run the streets all night long or are you going to walk the paths of glory in his sunshine? Are you going to twerk or are you going to trust God? Are you going to be racked with cowardice, or are you going to be powered by commitment? It's time to make up your mind, to rededicate yourself to God while times are good, to give God glory while the battle is raging, to praise him while the race is being run. It is time to reset.

Radiate the truth that God has been too good to you!

REFLECTIONS

- Purification requires separation. What are the things God is calling you to separate yourself from in order to enjoy the full fruits of your reset?
- Are you caught between Shechem and Bethel, or can you honestly say you have left Shechem behind?
- Meditate on where the Lord found you, and where he might take you.
- Where, honestly, is God on your list of priorities?

CHAPTER 6

LET GOD REINVENT YOU AND YOUR WORLD

Each of us has a mission. It may be simple and straight-forward, it may be far-reaching with many elements, but in becoming followers of Christ, each of us is called into his service in the way that will fit us best. It is a way designed to take advantage of our talents, our personalities, our particular gifts. There are vocations we are called to, roles we play in the lives of others, acts of kindness to be carried out, social good to be done, missions to undertake, and the gospel to share.

Each of us also has within us a sense of discernment concerning where God is taking us. That discernment, that sense of mission, may have been obscured along the way. We may have issues, we may have complicated pasts, but all of us have a sense of God's calling. And if we are embracing and pursuing that calling, we may face difficulties beyond the challenges of the task itself. It's hard to find people we can share our callings with. When you know there is something unique about you, and you know God has his hand on you, sharing that can provoke the insecurities of people around you. One of the lessons that comes with being reset is that there are times when it's best just to go on and do what we are called to do, no matter the reactions of people we know, even those closest to us.

Discernment
[is our]
sense of
our mission.

God's call to reset is part of realigning yourself to undertake your mission, and not everyone may understand it. But to be reset is to embrace your role as a visionary, a dreamer, a destiny chaser. You are called to embrace that whether or not people understand or support you.

Reset: Noah

Then the LORD saw that the wickedness of man was great in the earth, and that every intent of the thoughts of his heart was only evil continually. And the LORD was sorry that He had made man on the earth, and He was grieved in His heart. So the LORD said, "I will destroy man whom I have created from the face of the earth, both man and beast, creeping thing and birds of the air, for I am sorry that I have made them." But Noah found grace in the eyes of the LORD.

—GENESIS 6:5–8

Lest you think reset is only for those who have fallen to low stations, remember that we have seen that it is not a matter of station at all. Those who preach may be as in need of reset as those who listen, those whose wrongs are minor as much as those whose wrongs are great, those whose houses are in order as much as those whose houses are in chaos.

The call for reset, to be clear, is for those who are already among God's people. If you have no relationship with God, no channel of communication, something much more than reset is needed. That is the call to salvation, the call to be reborn. Reset is for those whose relationship with God already exists. It is a call to get back to that place where everything was fresh and firing on all cylinders.

Perhaps you have lost touch with the power and peace you found in Jesus early in your Christian walk, but you can still hear the voice of God calling you back. You may be far enough outside of God's will that you have fallen into a pit of despair. Or maybe you have just gone a little stale and have allowed other things to crowd out God.

Or perhaps you are solidly on the path, but you feel the call to something better, something bigger. Your walk with God may be as solid as ever, but you know there is more to strive for. God can turbocharge even the most committed believer and take him or her to heights they've never dreamed of. God can offer them new challenges that revolutionize their lives while enabling them to do great service to the people of God, the community, or the world as a whole.

God can turbocharge even the most committed believer.

Few people have had it more together than Noah. In fact, in an age of chaos it was Noah alone on God's team. "Noah was a righteous man," says Genesis 6:9 (ESV), while "the earth was corrupt in God's sight, and the earth was filled with violence" (v. 11 ESV).

It is likely that Noah was a farmer. In Genesis 5:29, we are told that Lamech, in naming his son Noah, said, "This one will comfort us concerning our work and the toil of our hands, because of the ground which the LORD has cursed." It's logical to think that in one sense he was saying Noah's labor would help take some of the burden from Lamech in tilling the soil.

More important, though, Noah was the one bright spot on an earth whose wickedness grieved God the Father. Such was the violence and degradation he saw everywhere that he vowed simply to destroy what he had made.

If it had not been for Noah, the human experiment might have ended right there. You and I might not be here. But Noah was "a just man, perfect in his generations. Noah walked with God" (6:9). And so God chose reset rather than destruction for the human race. He would save Noah and his family—eight people in all—as well as representatives of every kind of animal to begin repopulating the earth when the waters finally receded.

Lessons from the Flood

We can learn much about our own reset from the picture the Bible paints here. Through reset, we can leave the past behind. In the process of resetting us, God is erasing the past, wiping it out as if with a worldwide flood. We no longer have to be bound by the mistakes, the wreckage of our former selves. We can be free of those things that had held us in bondage and kept us separated from the will and power of God. We can emerge from the ark of reset into a new world, with each new sunrise in essence the first.

God wants us moving forward, not backward. He wants us concentrating on the future, not the past. With reset, failure is in the rearview mirror. God has called us to new challenges, and he will give us new strength to meet them. The world we enter once we reset is filled with hope and promise.

> We can emerge from the ark of reset into a new world.

· And what about Noah? That farmer, that man of God, was already possessed of a pure heart. He already had the desire to live for God. But now he would be repurposed. He would go from harvesting crops to harvesting timber. He would go from shaping plowshares to shaping an ark. He would go from tilling the ground to sailing the waters.

With the planetary reset, everything changed. The rains that had once nourished the earth now destroyed it. Just the faithful remnant of humanity would remain. Noah's reset would in essence be that of humanity, since he and his family were all that remained.

Noah had already stayed faithful within the storm that roiled the earth in the form of wantonly destructive human behavior. He was steadfast when all else was chaos. Now he would face a literal worldwide storm.

As he had on the ground, though, Noah would be traveling with God. He would utilize skills he had honed all his life. No doubt as a farmer he had worked with animals, and that experience would serve him well on an ark filled with them. God told him to gather food for his family and the animals, and no doubt much of that came from his farm.

God does not erase the good in you when he resets you. He just allows you to clear away the dross that keeps you from using that goodness, those skills, for his purpose. He will continue to use your talents and attributes.

That is what reset did for Noah. It is what it will do for you.

Peter: Rescued, Retooled, Restored

Immediately Jesus made His disciples get into the boat and go before Him to the other side, while He sent the multitudes away. And when He had sent the multitudes away, He went up on the mountain by Himself to pray. Now when evening came, He was alone there. But the boat was now in the middle of the sea, tossed by the waves, for the wind was contrary.

Now in the fourth watch of the night Jesus went to them, walking on the sea. And when the disciples saw Him walking on the sea, they were troubled, saying, "It is a ghost!" And they cried out for fear.

But immediately Jesus spoke to them, saying, "Be of good cheer! It is I; do not be afraid."

And Peter answered Him and said, "Lord, if it is You, command me to come to You on the water."

So He said, "Come." And when Peter had come down out of the boat, he walked on the water to go to Jesus. But when he saw that the wind was boisterous, he was afraid; and beginning to sink he cried out, saying, "Lord, save me!"

And immediately Jesus stretched out His hand and caught him, and said to him, "O you of little faith, why did you doubt?" And when they got into the boat, the wind ceased.

—MATTHEW 14:22–32

Of all the examples of people who were reset in the Bible, few are worth studying more than Peter. No one got more personal attention from Jesus. No one seemed to have more potential as a leader, and no one seemed to struggle more. He experienced incredible highs and unfathomable lows. Nobody shows more clearly what being reset really means.

Peter spent three years, day in and day out, with the Lord, and it was Peter to whom Jesus entrusted his young church. Peter and his brother, Andrew, were the first people called to be disciples. He was with Jesus at pivotal moments from the transfiguration to the garden of Gethsemane. It was Peter who first realized and said, "You are the Christ" (Matt. 16:16). And yet after all that, Peter denied even knowing Jesus. Along the way Jesus retooled him, rescued him, rebuked him, and restored him.

What kind of man was Peter? Why is he someone we can identify with so easily? Peter was hardworking, plainspoken, and definitely earthy. As a fisherman he would have been possessed of great strength and stamina. He was impetuous and yet he could be solid and trustworthy once he was on board with something. Jesus called him a rock, as a nod to that core of stability, yet Jesus knew as well as anyone that Peter could fly off the handle and be driven off-course by anger or fear. His impulsiveness had its positive aspects—he impulsively left his boats to follow Jesus, for instance. He was so human, so fallible, and yet so dogged and determined.

For all Peter's flaws, Jesus knew that at Peter's core he was special, and Jesus entrusted him with leadership the way God has entrusted you with your own mission. One of the pivotal moments in Peter's life provides us with a great example of the ability and willingness to follow Jesus no matter what the level of support or understanding from others. In this story from Matthew, Jesus sent the disciples ahead of him in a ship while he went to a mountaintop to pray and talk to the Father. The disciples, on the boat by themselves, experienced fierce winds and waves that beat against the ship. No doubt they had to work hard just to keep the boat righted.

During the fourth watch—between 3:00 a.m. and 6:00 a.m.—Jesus began walking toward them on that choppy water. This was an intense storm, the kind that is still common on the Sea of Galilee, but the storm is also a fitting symbol of the spiritual, emotional, and mental upheavals the disciples were going through and that we go through as well. Jesus had just been rejected by the people of his hometown of Nazareth. Then his cousin John the Baptist was beheaded. Now the apostles, in this storm-tossed boat at three in the morning, saw a figure walking toward them on the water. They made the perfectly logical assumption that it was a ghost, and they were terrified.

Jesus called out, "Be of good cheer! It is I; do not be afraid" (14:27). *It's okay! Be cool.* Sometimes in the worst of our own storms, when we're wondering where the Lord is, he has a way of reminding us that he's right in the middle of it with us.

Come On

One of the things that made Peter special was his impetuous desire for the good stuff. He wanted to be in the midst of things. He wanted to be key to the mission. On this rainy, windy night, he was about to exemplify courage. Keep in mind that all the disciples were on that ship, but it was Peter who said, "Lord, if it is you, then bid me to come. Let me walk on the water" (v. 28, author's paraphrase). He was the one with the faith to believe it was possible. The lesson for us is striking. There will be plenty of people who have the opportunity to hear God's call, who are called to reset. It is up to you to be Peter, the one who says, "If there's a chance to walk on water, I'll take it."

Jesus, without hesitation, called him. "Come on," he said. The Lord wants us to stretch, wants us to work miracles, wants us to reach for the thing others are afraid to try. He'll tell us that if we'll just listen.

Peter got out of that boat and began doing something that had never been done before by anyone who wasn't God. He began to walk on water. A storm was raging. All of the apostles were on the ship, and all but one were still living in their fear. Peter asked, and Jesus gave him the opportunity to show just what he was made of.

God will set things up for you that way sometimes, presenting a seemingly impossible situation for just that purpose—to see what you're made of. God is looking for you to reveal who you really are. He's giving you the chance to step up and live out the assignment that is made just for you, that calls on your skills and takes on a task other people might well think you're crazy for taking on.

"You're going back to school?" "You're going after *that*

job?" "You're going on a mission trip?" "You want to buy a house?" That's what you might well hear from your friends and family when you go after the next goal, the next dream in your life. And that may well have been what Peter's eleven brothers in the boat were thinking or saying when Peter stepped out to walk on the surface of the sea.

> [God is] giving you the chance to step up and live out the assignment that is made just for you.

You're not called to be like everybody else. God will give you things to do that other people might not get on board with. Sometimes if you talk to people about it, you just might turn a friend into a hater, so you may want keep it to yourself. Notice that Peter did not form a committee or poll the other apostles. He spoke directly to Jesus.

If you're going to dream and dare big things, I have news for you: you're going to have to leave some people in the ship. Wrap your mind around the fact that you cannot worry about the opinions and attitudes of people who stay behind. When you know God has called you to do something, those opinions don't matter. There's no need to seek approval from people who aren't going where you're trying to go.

The Ships We Ride In

There are certain ships in life we all ride in—relation*ships*, friend*ships*, partner*ships*, fellow*ships*. And some of those ships are too small to get you where God is taking you. These ships can't always hold the massive vision God has for your life. When your calling is bigger than the ship you are in, it's time to step out into the water, even if it's stormy. Certain systems and organizations and corporations are designed to keep you at a certain level, to hold you down and keep you in your place. You may feel the pressure. You may have been thinking, *Wait a minute! I know there is something in me that is bigger than this ship and the constraints it places on me.*

Sometimes you have to say, "I love you, ship, but I've got to go. You've brought me this far, but you're just too small to take me where I'm going." Sometimes the ships people want you to get into are too small. They become places of containment that cause you to get stuck and to fail to reach your destination.

God is moving you out of those small places. God is taking you to a place, where, in communion with him, you can find the power to walk on water. Dr. Martin Luther King Jr. drew on the image of the mountain—Mt. Nebo, in this case, where Moses was granted a view of the promised land—in his last speech, given in Memphis on April 3, 1968. This is the speech known for the phrase, "I have been to the mountaintop." And it is interesting to note that Dr. King opened his remarks that evening thanking people for attending the rally "in spite of a storm warning," something with both literal and richly metaphorical meanings. In his remarks he was declaring that because he had been to the mountaintop, he refused to be limited by the systematic oppression of the age, and he was able to step out of complacency to receive strength and do something that had never been done before.

I've been there, Dr. King was saying, and it isn't about me. If I don't get there, it doesn't matter, as long as you get there.

> God is moving you out of those small places.

Are You Ready to Step Out?

When you step out of the boat, you're declaring, "It isn't about me." Like Jesus, like Moses, like everybody God has ever used, it's never about you but what God can accomplish through you. And if you're going to ask God to give you the ability to step out of the boat, you had better be prepared to step out. Don't ask for it if you aren't ready for it. Peter made his request. "Lord, since you say it's you, can I come?" Jesus said, "Come on," with no hesitation and no reservation.

You would think there might have been a pause, some examination of Peter, a determination that he was mentally ready. But Jesus already knew Peter was ready. He knew he would be the one. The Lord knows your level of readiness. He knows how prepared you are. And it's up to you to know that you have too much of the Word in you not to be ready.

Are you ready to step out into what God has called you to do? Don't let people with boat mentality keep you from your destiny. You cannot allow others to make that determination, and it's not just what they are doing now that we're talk-

The Lord knows your level of readiness.

ing about. Look past what they have done and don't worry about what they might do to you. Don't give them the power to hinder your progress.

Peter had little regard for the opinions of those who didn't have the faith to step out with him. He stepped out of the boat. Boat mentality is the province of those who are content with settling for systems that limit their potential. It is the province of those who would rather trust the safety of a boat without Jesus than step out and trust the sea with Jesus. These are people who would rather be content with being confined to the *comforts* of the boat—even if the boat is crowded, noisy, smelly, and leaking—than risk walking on water. They are unwilling to move out and trust God for what God is getting ready to do.

You know those kinds of people. You've seen them. They don't want to do anything, and they don't want anybody else to do anything. They're the folk you see when you go back to your old neighborhood or your hometown, sitting on the stoop talking nonsense. They're lifetime crew members on a boat going nowhere. Aren't you glad you got out of the boat? Aren't you glad you said, "Hey, that's not for me." That's what Abraham did, that's what Jacob did, and that's what Peter did. They said, "God is calling me to something greater, and I'm willing to go."

I am not telling you to act stuck-up, like you're better

than other people. But you know you've outgrown people on the boat when you start having conversations with them and they're talking about the boat and you're talking about the sea and they don't understand what you're talking about. You're talking about your future. They're talking about your history. You're talking about where you're going. They're talking about where you've been.

Another Level of Faith

Remember, it takes faith to walk on water—another level of faith altogether. Second Corinthians 5:7 says, "For we walk by faith, not by sight." Walking on a stormy sea is not for wimps. Trust God to keep you in an environment you've never walked in. I always tell people, "Don't step out if you don't have the faith to stick it out." There's a reason some people stay in the boat. They lack the faith or fortitude to chart new courses. They would rather walk in somebody else's footprints than create their own.

Be determined to accept the challenges that are inevitably going to come. You can't commit to the sea if you're not willing to go all the way. It's going to take time with God to prepare yourself to walk on water. That's why we need that time on the mountain, in prayer and communion with God. What's more, you had better count the cost. Nehemiah understood this. When he got confirmation from the king that it was time to build the walls of Jerusalem, he told his people working with him, "I need you to have building materials in one hand and a weapon in the other, because we got a word from the king" (see Neh. 4:16).

When you get a word from the King, it doesn't matter who doesn't like you or who's trying to come against you. You just walk out there. Why did Peter step out of the boat? Because the King told him to. It doesn't matter who was in the boat talking. If God told you to do it, you have to do it.

Don't expect even those closest to you to understand. Peter was out there by himself. The disciples were still in the boat. If you're not comfortable with some isolation, if you can't deal with being misunderstood, if you can't handle a hater or two making things up about you, if you can't take criticism, then you may want to stay in the boat. It can be lonely out there. But what you gain when you step out of the boat is the presence of Jesus, and if you have him, that's all you need. He is the cure for that loneliness. I would much rather have Jesus and me in a storm than me and eleven frightened people in the boat.

> I would much rather have me and Jesus in a storm than me and eleven frightened people in the boat.

Your Destination, Not Your Situation

Once you have the willingness, once you've counted the cost, success in any endeavor involves keeping your eye on your destination, not your situation. If you're going to make it, it's critical that you maintain focus. People don't always give Peter enough credit. He walked on water! But as he experienced the rising waves and the howling winds, he took his eyes off of Jesus. He was on his way to meet Jesus on the surface of a stormy sea, and then he got in his own head. He became so distracted by his current situation that he forgot about his ultimate destination.

Some of you are looking at what you're going *through*, and you've taken your eyes off of where you're going *to*. You've forgotten that when the Lord said, "Come" to Peter, and to you, he had already factored in the things that were going to happen. He knew what stood between where you had been and where you were going. And in the case of Peter, the Jesus walking toward him was the very God who had made the wind and the waves in the first place. He was in control then, and he's in control now.

If your trust is in Jesus, and Jesus has called you to walk on water, wind and waves are not going to take you out. Understand who is in control of your situation. Make up your mind that nothing is going to keep you from the promise of God. It's a matter of saying, "I'm going to get what God has for my life."

What God shows us when Peter falters is that he rescues us from failing situations. The text says Peter lost focus and began to sink. He cried out to the Lord, and the Lord took him by the hand and lifted him up. You have to realize that God is committed to your reaching your destination. All of us have failed at one time or another. Some people you know may act like they've never taken their eyes off of Jesus, but all of us, if we're honest, will admit that we have. All of us have doubted. All of us have failed. If it were not for the grace of God, none of us would be here today. When the worst was about to happen, God *stepped in* and rescued us.

Peter was walking toward Jesus, and we can assume that Jesus was walking toward Peter. Jesus was destined to get to Peter before he reached the boat. I'm fascinated by what that tells me—Jesus gets to people on the sea before he gets to the people in the boat. When you fall, Jesus is as close to you as he is to the people cowering on the boat. The other thing I think is fascinating is that when Peter slipped, he cried out to Jesus, which is a deeper revelation to me. He didn't call out to the others in the boat. And when he slipped, you would assume that one of the boys he'd been rolling with would have said, "Let's help Peter!" But if people don't have the faith to step out with you in the first place, what makes you think they're going to come to your rescue when you're in trouble? I'm not putting my faith in people. I put my faith in Jesus. That's who I'm calling on.

Falling Isn't Failing

It's worth noting too that the closer you get to your destination, the greater your distraction. The waves may well have been getting bigger as Peter walked toward Jesus. Think of your own situation, the times when you said, "I've been out here for a while. Why now, God, has the storm grown like this?" It's because the Enemy knows this is his last chance to derail you before you arrive at your destination. It's gotten rougher because you're closer now than you've ever been. This isn't the time to whine. This is the time to shout, to say, "Lord, thank you because I wouldn't be going through all these distractions if I were not close to my destination." Every distraction is confirmation that you're close.

Peter teaches us that falling doesn't make us a failure and that we don't have to be defined by our falls. That's one reason we shouldn't be hard on the Peters of the world when they mess up. There's some Peter in all of us, and I come against the judgmental spirit that wants to look down at those who falter. Everybody has failed at something. If you haven't, keep on living, and you will.

Some widely quoted sayings about failure have been attributed to some well-known men: Robert Kennedy— "Only those who dare to fail greatly can ever achieve greatly." Winston Churchill—"Success is not final, failure is not fatal. It is the courage to continue that counts." C. S. Lewis—"Failures are finger posts on the road to achievement. One fails forward toward success." Abraham Lincoln—"My great concern is not whether you have failed, but whether you are content with failure." And Zig Ziglar—"Remember, failure is an event, not a person."

> Peter teaches us that falling doesn't make us a failure.

You should never give up on people who fail because the

kingdom is full of them. It's full of people who failed but got back up. Maybe you're one of them. Maybe, like Peter, you blew it. You stepped out there and were doing it, but then things got rough, and you lost focus and fell. But God gave you another chance. The Bible says Jesus took Peter by the hand, and they walked back to the boat. Maybe people were ready to count you out, but I am here to tell you, you are not a failure because you fail. It's not over until God says it's over, and if you have nothing else to praise God for, thank God that you are not defined by your slipups but by your pickups. You are defined by where God is getting ready to take you.

Called to Carry On

Whether it's your career, marriage, health, ministry, or education, God is not interested in letting you go under. The Bible says Peter was beginning to sink, but he did not go all the way under. He called out to Jesus, and Jesus took him by the hand. I don't care what has happened in your life; God is not going to let you go under. He responds to the cries of his children. Because you had the courage to step out on a word from God, because you did what nobody else had the courage to do, because you walked on water, God said, "I am invested in your future." You are called to success. You may have lost focus, but Jesus rescued you.

I was sinking deep in sin, far from the
*   peaceful shore,*
Very deeply stained within, sinking to rise no
*   more,*
But the Master of the sea heard my
*   despairing cry,*
From the waters lifted me, now safe am I.
Love lifted me!
    —JAMES ROWE, "LOVE LIFTED ME"

When Peter and Jesus got back to the ship, the other disciples said, "Now we know you're the son of God" (Matt. 14:33, author's paraphrase), and they began to praise him. God is going to make your haters understand who he is.

Some people speculate on how far Peter sank before he cried out. Some say he was ankle-deep. Some say he was waist-deep. Some say he sank up to his neck. I don't know how far Peter sank, but I have a revelation for you. No matter how deep you're in it, if you're alive, God has kept your head above water, and as long as your head is above water, you can cry out to Jesus. You may be neck-deep in your relationship, in your career, in your marriage, in your finances. But as long as you can get a word out to the Master, your breakthrough is at hand.

There is no reason to hang your head because of the tough times. You might feel like giving up, but God is not going to let you go under. You might be the only one in your family doing what you're doing. You might be the

As long as your head is above water, you can cry out to Jesus.

only one in your bloodline who has stepped outside the boat, and that's why the devil is trying to kill you. But I don't care how high the water is. It's not over your head because it's under his feet.

What God has for you is too big for you to remain in that small ship. God is about to release you. Step out, even if you have to step out by yourself. God is not going to let you go. Every day you may pass by doubters and people who don't get it. They are the people still in the boat.

I don't talk to boat people anymore. I talk to people like you. Go after your destiny. Get what God has for you. Get your degree. Get your house. Become debt-free. Write that book. Go after it. I'm looking for water-walkers, people who can say, "Even if I've got to walk by myself, I'm going to walk. God is not going to let me go."

Get out of the boat.

Reset and Repurpose

The world has its own kinds of resets. Graduation, a new job, marriage, parenthood, and many other milestones that carry new status or responsibilities are seen in the world as resets. They are rites of passage analogous in a limited way to the spiritual resets we are talking about—and sometimes they are one and the same.

Often one of the marks of such a reset is a name change. We see it in marriage. We see it in professional titles, such as doctor, pastor, or lieutenant. Family relations can do it. All of a sudden, daddy, mommy, grandma, uncle, and aunt are names that indicate a new relation or status. There are other examples. Monarchs and popes often take new names upon assuming their new roles, and many actors, musicians, and others in the public eye rebrand themselves with names that indicate they are stepping into new roles.

We have already seen some biblical examples of name changes, and it's worth revisiting Peter, to examine the way his identity was changed by Jesus, as we examine the way our own identities and labels shift when we undergo the spiritual reset we are aiming for with this book. As in the case of Jacob and Abram, a name change indicates the profound turnaround to which these people were called. They were given new identities, signaling new mission and purpose.

Simon Peter: The Rock

He said to them, "But who do you say that I am?" Simon Peter answered and said, "You are the Christ, the Son of the living God." Jesus answered and said to him, "Blessed are you, Simon Bar-Jonah, for flesh and blood has not revealed this to you, but My Father who is in heaven. And I also say to you that you are Peter,

and on this rock I will build My church, and the gates
of Hades shall not prevail against it.

—MATTHEW 16:15–18

We looked at the life and lessons of Peter in an earlier
chapter, but let's stop for a moment to look at his transformation. John 1 tells us that Jesus met this fisherman
named Simon through his brother, Andrew, and renamed
him right then and there—*Cephas*, or Peter, meaning
"stone" or "rock"—so the story in Matthew is most likely
a reaffirmation.

Let's revisit Peter in all his complexity. We looked in
detail at the fact that he was trusting enough to ask Jesus to
let him walk on water and then self-conscious and doubt-
ful enough to lose focus and sink. He was weak enough to
fall asleep in Gethsemane when the Lord asked him to wait
up with him, then impetuous enough to slice an ear from
the high priest's servant. He was cocky enough to boast
he would never betray Jesus, then craven enough to deny
knowing him three separate times. His reaction to the last
event, though, is a key to Peter. He wept bitterly when he
was caught in his own duplicity and weakness, for he loved
the Lord and hated the part of himself that could be weak
and cowardly.

Jesus knew and loved the complex human being that was
Peter. At the Last Supper, he said, "Simon, Simon, behold,
Satan has demanded permission to sift you like wheat; but
I have prayed for you, that your faith may not fail; and you,

when once you have turned again, strengthen your brothers" (Luke 22:31–32 NASB). He knew the depths and the heights of which Peter was capable. He knew the denial was coming, but he knew too that once the disciples would be on their own, following his departure, Peter would be the one who could lead. "Be the rock, as I have named you," Jesus was saying to him, and there would soon come a time when Jesus would say to Peter, "Feed my lambs. Feed my sheep" (John 21:15, 17).

But it is the episode in Matthew where Jesus renamed him that lets us see both Peter and his relationship with Jesus in all their complexity. It was Peter who took the lead in answering Jesus' question: "But who do you say I am?" His knowledge, Jesus assured him, was not his own. It was divine. Peter had crossed a huge threshold in his discipleship. He was drawing on the things of heaven. As the time grew shorter, Peter was seeing more. He was still Peter—there was plenty more weakness ready to show through—but God was entrusting him with insights not granted to everyone else.

Peter: The Highs and the Lows

From that time Jesus began to show to His disciples that He must go to Jerusalem, and suffer many things from the elders and chief priests and scribes, and be killed, and be raised the third day.

—MATTHEW 16:21

Just how much of the old Peter was still there was evident in his very next exchange with Jesus. Jesus began to talk about the suffering he would soon face and about the fact that he would be killed. It was Peter, rash as ever, who reacted first. You can just see him grabbing Jesus' arm and taking him off to the side.

"Far be it from You, Lord," he said. "This shall not happen to You!" (Matt. 16:22).

Jesus didn't get angry often, but when he did, people wilted.

"Get behind Me, Satan!" he said, no doubt shocking Peter and all the rest. "You are an offense to Me, for you are not mindful of the things of God, but the things of men" (v. 23). This is the leader of the apostles, being upbraided as clueless in the moments after God had given him the keys to the kingdom!

In Peter we see the highest highs and the lowest lows of discipleship, and it's worth asking why Jesus stayed with him. "Peter," we can hear him saying, "the reason I never gave up on you is because I knew I needed your special attributes. Yes, I said, 'The devil wants to sift you like wheat.' I saw your deficiencies. I knew your proclivities. I knew all your issues, and yet I loved you through it all. I knew you were called to be the one. Peter, you often had your brain in park and your mouth in drive. You always wanted to give me advice; you always did crazy things. You were just a rough-around-the-edges guy, but I saw something in you, Peter, and even when you left me when things got tough, I never gave up on you because I always believed in you. I saw in you the capacity to discern and interpret spiritually what the other disciples could not."

The Holy Spirit bestowed on Peter the gifts he needed. He was not a rock on his own. He was shifting sand, sometimes faithful, sometimes faithless. He ran hot and cold, depending on the circumstances. With the Holy Spirit, though, Peter became the stabilizing influence for the new church and living proof that God always believes in those he has called.

Peter became the foundation through which the church emerged. He was the defender of Pentecost. This shows us clearly that being reset is a gift that we must meet halfway, applying ourselves to facing and rising above our own weakness and shortsightedness. And we can't forget that God uses us because he needs our special gifts. He needs us as his eyes and ears and as his mouthpiece. As members of the body of Christ, we have roles that only we can play.

Mary Magdalene

And the twelve were with Him, and certain women who had been healed of evil spirits and infirmities— Mary called Magdalene, out of whom had come seven demons, and Joanna the wife of Chuza, Herod's steward, and Susanna, and many others who provided for Him from their substance.

—LUKE 8:1–3

Our final look at reinvention in this chapter comes with Mary Magdalene. The only pre-crucifixion mention of her in Scripture references the seven demons cast out of her by Jesus. We don't know if their manifestation was behavioral or a physical or mental illness. It is through references in apocryphal writings that we get the picture of her as someone who had led a life of sin, probably in prostitution, until meeting Jesus. In any case, her association with Jesus reinvented her, and Mary (the name *Magdalene* simply refers to her as a native of Magdala, on the Sea of Galilee) was apparently close to Jesus for the rest of his ministry on earth and with his followers after that. What's clear is that she was profoundly changed and carried her gratitude into loyalty and service, most likely for the rest of her life.

It is with the events of the crucifixion that Mary Magdalene comes into sharper focus in the gospels. First of all, her mere presence at this Roman execution spectacle was testament to her bravery and steadfastness since the apostles, with the exception of John, had by this time run off. She and another Mary were present when Jesus was laid in the tomb and lingered after its owner, Joseph of Arimathea, left. She was at the tomb Sunday morning. and both John and Mark say she was the first person to see the risen Christ.

Mary Magdalene is generally named first among the women who followed Jesus, the way Peter is named first when the apostles are named, indicating that she had more than likely assumed a leadership role, and the phrase "provided for Him from their substance" may well mean she contributed financially as well. Whatever her past, Mary Magdalene's life with Jesus is a great representation of transformation, love, and service.

How Does It Feel to Be Reset?

To be reset is to be hauled into a master's studio as a block of granite, nothing more than potential, and emerge as Michelangelo's *David*; it is to lie on a palette as daubs of color and come to life on canvas as Da Vinci's *The Last Supper*.

To be reset is to go into the furnace as oblong clay, wet and glistening, soft, no more than mud, and emerge as a brick, a useful building tool, ready to be part of a great structure.

To be reset is to go into the locker room at halftime trailing, downtrodden, and with defeat in your heart, and emerge for the second half on fire, with nothing but victory in your heart, willing to do whatever it takes to operate at the absolute peak of your capacity.

To be reset is to go into boot camp an aimless youth, a little soft, a lot unfocused, and emerge a soldier, someone honed and hardened, someone with clear purpose and a new sense of pride and character.

To be reset is to be broken eggs that reemerge as a soufflé.

To be reset is to be hauled from the junkyard as a rusty old automobile, broken-down, unable to do that for which you were made, and emerge from a reconditioner's shop gleaming, running smooth as a purring tiger, ready to take to the road or to dazzle at a vintage auto show.

To be reset is to be an orphan, abandoned by someone whose life is in ruin, and emerge later from an adoptive household a healthy, happy human being, ready for a life of use and value.

To be reset is to be a yolk and white inside a shell, basically just a blob of gelled liquid, to be absorbed by a tiny single-celled embryo and grow to become a fully formed chick, cracking that shell from the inside and emerging as a fledgling, ready for the world.

To be reset is to be an abandoned property with weeds and thickets all over the yard, the house closed up and musty in need of repair, and emerge a showplace, with fresh paint and sunlight streaming in, the yard trimmed along with hedges and gardens and a glistening pool in the back.

Blessing in a Bottle

Shakespeare wrote of sermons in stones, and this is the story of my blessing in a bottle.

I was thirsty one day, and I picked up a plastic bottle of water. I say humorously sometimes that inanimate objects talk to me, and this one certainly did. As I was about to open it, my spirit heard it say, "Hey, before you open me and drink me, I need to tell you my story."

"Okay," I said. "Tell me your story."

"Well," it said, "one day not long ago, someone turned me up and emptied me. I'm not nearly as thick as some plastic containers, and I'm certainly not as hard as glass, and this person crushed me until I was flat and tossed me in the trash. I was misshapen, dirty, and surrounded by garbage. Not a great place to be, is it?"

"I should say not."

"But then someone came along and spied me and recognized that I have value. She lifted me out of that place of darkness and despair and took me with her. I didn't know where I was going, but I was glad to be out of where I was. She tossed me into a bin, where I recognized that everyone around me was a lot like me. We were still dented and in some cases dirty, but someone had recognized that all of us had value. We wound up in a recycling plant, where we were cleaned up, re-formed, and made brand-new again. I went to a place where they filled me with water and—voilà—here I am."

Like that bottle, I've been recycled. That's my story. I have been reborn to do great things. That can be your story too. It doesn't matter where you've been or what you've done. It doesn't matter if you wound up on life's trash heap. Our God is a recycler—the Great Recycler. His people haven't always been what they are now. He's poured out our pasts and purified us as he's refilled us and sent us out into the world.

REFLECTIONS

- What is your mission? What is it that God has called you to do?
- Can you imagine reset as a clean break with what doesn't work in your past, a rebooting as profound as the Great Flood?
- How do you identify with Peter? Share a time when you or someone you know acted like Peter.
- How do the "ships" in your life—relationships, friendships, and so on—serve you well or badly?
- Are you ready to trust Jesus outside of the boat?

CHAPTER 7

RESURRECTION: THE GREAT RESET

The greatest reset in history is the one at the core of Christianity. It is the resurrection of Jesus. That is the point at which darkness turned to light, defeat to victory, death to life. Victory was in hand. Forgiveness was ours. The door to heaven locked by Adam's sin was opened.

It was a reset for all of humanity, made possible by the reset Jesus undertook, first, in becoming human and then in dying in our stead, taking on all the sins of human history, and finally in overcoming death, rising on Easter Sunday so we might live.

There is no bigger moment. There is no more profound reset. It makes all the others possible, and we share in the full power of the resurrection with every recommitment to God and to the mission he has assigned each of us.

The lessons of reset are there for the taking in the story

of Christ's passion. After all, Jesus was fully human as well as fully divine, and he experienced the same range of emotions we would experience in the face of such an overwhelming task.

My Leadership Journey

And He sat down, called the twelve, and said to them, "If anyone desires to be first, he shall be last of all and servant of all."

—MARK 9:35

There is nothing multiple-choice about taking Jesus as a role model. We can't pick and choose among the traits he held up for us to follow. That's especially true for those of us who preach his Word. Jesus could hold an audience spellbound with his preaching; he could heal; he could perform miracles; but anyone who looks at his brilliance and his power must be struck above all by his love and his humility. They are the background against which all the rest stands out even more starkly. Love is the bottom line, and without it, as Paul says, the world's best preaching is as a clanging gong.

Jesus reserved his earthly wrath for those who were hypocrites, for those in church leadership positions who did not display the spirit of love and humility he expected from those of us who serve him—especially those of us who serve him in the pulpit and in the ministry.

If you would be first, be a servant.

There are challenges faced by any preacher, and one of the biggest lies in the way leaders are treated. Ours is a culture of celebrity and, like it or not, anyone in the public eye on any level, from local to international, feels the pull of it. Athletes, performers, news anchors, politicians, and, yes, even preachers find that things change when they become highly visible. That culture of celebrity is a snare. It feeds the ego, and the ego is not the proper source of love for others.

If you would be first, be a servant.

I was in my twenties when the church I pastor started growing. At first, maybe one hundred people a week saw me in the pulpit. Before long that number was in the thousands. We started a television ministry, and people who never set foot in the church knew my name and heard my preaching. I was emerging as a leader. That's when I looked around and first saw for myself how people make celebrities out of those in the public eye.

No one who is human can be totally immune to the lure of being noticed, being praised, being recognized for one's accomplishments. But therein lies a problem. Those who make celebrities of people in the public eye see only the public person. No one who is human is wholly good or completely praiseworthy. In my case, those who saw me on television, saw me immersed in the Word of God, excited about sharing it, at my best doing something I love. They didn't see me in my off moments, when things were going wrong.

The celebrity me wasn't the real me. The celebrity me was a cultural construct. That's not to say it wasn't flattering, but it was not a path I could embrace and still hope to remain where God was leading me. That's why levelheaded people in the public eye crave the company of those who knew them when, who can call them on their behavior when it seems as if the praise is going to their head.

Reset to Authenticity

The bigger the church grew, the bigger the phenomenon became. I began writing books. I started to be recognized in airports in other cities. Then when I was named presiding bishop of an international movement, I realized my photograph was appearing in media outlets around the world. It's bracing stuff. The temptations toward pride and ego were intense. I had to fight them.

My personal call to reset at that time was toward a spirit of humility. That's what the Spirit was calling me to—authenticity, the place where I was me, without filters, without any magnification or amplification.

What was my path to be?

First, I had to understand what was happening. The process of becoming a celebrity is not about granting you freedom. It's the culture's way of imprisoning you within an image. Ask those people who try to break out and rebrand themselves. The media is invested in categorization. They want to control the image—your image.

Second, I had to understand the truth I was aiming for.

A celebrity status was attempting to put barriers between me and people. That, I realized, was the key to resisting it. I had to make sure I stayed connected to people. Celebrity is impersonal. Integrity is relational. I had to choose to redefine what leadership looked like in my case. I realized it was based in walking among the people. To stay connected to people, I had to stay connected to my authentic self. I had to preach what I preached, and teach what I taught.

Third, I had to know the stakes. To succumb to celebrity status would be to lose my authenticity, to trade in who I am for a bit of reputational bling, to trade God for mammon. What people need now is not another ecclesiastical celebrity. They need someone who can walk alongside them when the road is rocky and steep. People have walked alongside me through the most difficult times—theirs and mine—and I know what is important. It's that touch. It's two or more gathering in Jesus' name. It's people following his command to love one another as he has loved us.

And fourth, I had to know the process. I had to fight every single day against the spirit of pride. Being reset involves recommitting every morning to this new approach.

I had to decide whether I wanted to go down the road toward becoming the next big thing, toward becoming a celebrity, or whether I wanted

> What people need now is not another ecclesiastical celebrity. They need someone who can walk alongside them when the road is rocky and steep.

to be the person who impacts people at the ground level, relationally.

Jesus impacted people relationally throughout his ministry. He continues to do that, in the hearts of everyone who follows him. His approach grew out of his knowledge of his mission. Jesus said, "I have come . . . to do . . . the will of Him who sent Me" (John 6:38). That's ultimately how I want to live, and that is the choice I made.

"The Word became flesh and dwelt among us" (1:14). Jesus chose to come down and dwell among people who would ultimately turn on him and kill him. He lived with those whose sins he would bear on the cross. So who am I that I can't walk among people?

That is the essence of reset for me.

Ministry and Family

Another reset involved my priorities. It was about acknowledging that there is often a tension between ministry and family. The hustle and bustle of ministry can swell into pathology. It can become burdensome. Ministry wants all your time. The church ministry is a jealous mistress, and it has destroyed many homes.

I had to look at my situation. I have a wife and a daughter, and one look in my daughter's eyes tells me how much she loves her daddy. As a husband and father, I had to ask, "Where are my priorities?" I had to recalibrate.

Reset for me meant not running around the country and leaving my family four times a week. I had to create a new paradigm, to bring my family with me and model togetherness as the goal.

When Abram received the word from God, "I will make you a great nation" (Gen. 12:2), God sent Abram to a new land, and he took Sarai, his wife, with him. God's calling was going to come to pass, and Abram's destiny was going to come to fruition with Sarai there by his side.

God is not going to ask me to abandon my family while he does his work through me. And I don't want my family to be bitter or resentful because I've left them behind. What is the point of my gaining success only to lose the very thing God gave me in the process?

> What is the point of my gaining success only to lose the very thing God gave me in the process?

Those two realizations helped recalibrate my ministry, and I believe God's voice is there both in my call to family and in my call to humility and relationship.

Resetting the Temple

> Or do you not know that your body is the temple of the Holy Spirit who is in you, whom you have from God, and you are not your own?
> —1 CORINTHIANS 6:19

Reset is by no means solely spiritual. The physical, emotional, and intellectual aspects of our lives matter as well.

Many people in the church, and in America in general, don't take proper care of themselves and neglect their health. I was no exception. As I traveled the country, I recognized how many people were feeding me fried chicken and collard greens and macaroni and cheese at eleven at night. I saw people singing in the choir, praising God, then getting on the elevator at one in the morning with greasy fast food bags in their hands. Eventually we were praying over these very same people because they were having heart failure. They were suffering from diabetes and hypertension and other preventable maladies.

God spoke to me about it. He said, "Son, you can change this. You can help change the way people view their bodies, as temples of the Holy Spirit." If you're not healthy, you can't fulfill your purpose.

Again, Jesus is the model. There's no doubt that the human Jesus was in great health. There is only once that we hear about him riding a donkey, and that was a ceremonial ride into Jerusalem at the beginning of the last week of his life. Instead, we hear a lot about Jesus walking. He and his disciples walked everywhere, and Jesus covered a lot of territory, much of it mountainous.

There is no way Jesus could have gone through the kind of excruciating torment he experienced under the Romans, carrying a three-hundred-pound cross up Golgotha's hill, had he not been in optimal health. It's something we don't often think about or comment on, but it's worth noting.

As a follower of Jesus, you can't ask God to increase your capacity, to expand your mission and enlarge your purpose, if you're not healthy enough to carry it out. You can't ask God to reset you and give you new challenges if you're not taking care of the very vessel he'll be using. Your physical health is a pretty basic foundation for everything else, and if he'll be using your body, you have to keep that body in optimal shape!

ChurchFit

Once I recognized that the fried chicken and mac and cheese had done their work on me, I knew it was time for a reset. God doesn't want me huffing and puffing while I preach. He wants me at the top of my game, and I have to take responsibility for that.

I started working out, watched what I ate, and lost thirty-five pounds. People saw what I was up to, saw the fitness modeled by my wife and me. They saw us being advocates for better health. We decided to take it a step further, knowing that the church is often the trusted cornerstone of the community. So we started ChurchFit, a comprehensive healthy lifestyle initiative designed to help people improve their health. We do it holistically, meaning we believe in strengthening the body in conjunction with the mind and spirit.

We offer classes and contests that focus on exercise, nutrition, and cooking, offering men and women the skills that can transform their lifestyles through healthy sustainable habits and endeavors.

Talk about a reset! ChurchFit swept through our church culture like wildfire. People started coming to classes, and they started exercising and eating right. We saw them change their entire mind-sets about their health, taking responsibility for their own well-being.

Now I feel better, just like they do. I can't tell you how good it feels when my wife wants something moved and rather than calling someone to come help me, I say, "I'll get that, dear!" I don't mind showing off my fitness just a little. Fitness also makes it easier to fulfill my purpose. I have more stamina and a greater ability to sustain my enthusiasm from the pulpit. If I'm running around doing seven services a week, preaching around the country at least three times a week—how can I do all that if I'm not healthy?

On a church level it's good to see people with BMI levels back to where they should be. I see people thanking God for renewed health and vigor. I hear fewer people talking about "my sugar diabetes" or "my high blood pressure" because more people are getting their health under control, often for the first time.

The devil wants to truncate your destiny by robbing you of your health, but the only way he can do that is if you're a willing participant. And I, for one, refuse to participate in suicide on the installment plan. Join me, and reset your life.

Surrender and Love

"But when he came to himself, he said, 'How many of my father's hired servants have bread enough and to spare, and I perish with hunger!' . . .

"And he arose and came to his father. But when he was still a great way off, his father saw him and had compassion, and ran and fell on his neck and kissed him."

—LUKE 15:17, 20

As we near the end of our journey, it is time to make sure we cast aside any lingering doubt and hesitation. There are those of you who've come this far with me in this book but who have let your intellect override your heart. Your fears have dampened your hope. Your weariness has reined in your dreams.

You hunger for reset but remain unconvinced that God can work with you. I know many people who believe God can do all things but don't believe God can do all things *for them.* They think they have wandered far enough from God that God is no longer interested.

Let us look at the case of the prodigal son. If ever there was an example for those of us who think we have strayed too far, who think we have stretched God's mercy past the breaking point, it is the prodigal son. If there is anyone who was an outcast and downcast because of his own actions, if there is anyone who might have fallen so low he doubted he could ever get back up, it was him.

We can guess what all he was into. Had he been a famous heir of our own age, any one of us could write the headlines, for we have seen it often—sex, drugs, alcohol, gambling, and all the rest of the craziness that goes with that lifestyle.

He burned through his portion of his father's estate. Then famine hit. The economy collapsed. He was broke and alone. He had burned every bridge, betrayed every friend, squandered every opportunity. There are rock stars who have squandered everything and wound up under bridges or living in their cars. But in this case there was an additional humiliating twist, for the prodigal son hired himself out to feed pigs. For Jews living during Jesus' day, no job could so sum up a great fall than that one, for pigs were unclean under Mosaic law. And he envied even the food of the pigs.

But then, in one of the great resets of the Bible, Jesus said, "He came to himself." He reentered his right mind. He surrendered.

The act of surrender amounts to saying, "I am done digging this hole." He no doubt heard the call we have talked about in this book, the call to sanity, to reunion with the father.

The prodigal son set a reset in motion by determining to return to his father, and he did so with all the humility we know is necessary.

> "How many of my father's hired servants have bread enough and to spare, and I perish with hunger! I will arise and go to my father, and will say to him, 'Father, I have sinned against heaven and before you, and I am no longer worthy to be called your son. Make me like one of your hired servants.'" (Luke 15:17–19)

He had turned his back once and for all on a lifestyle that had nearly killed him.

This young man had no money and no friends. He had no way to get a message to his father. He walked back home and prepared to offer himself as a servant in his father's household. He would wait tables, feed animals, do menial tasks, whatever it took to be back in the household where he grew up.

The act of surrender amounts to saying, "I am done digging this hole."

And we know what happened. His father reacted not with the vengeance the son might have expected but with love and compassion. He ran across the fields to him and welcomed him home. Then he told his servants to "put a ring on his hand and sandals on his feet. And bring the fatted calf here and kill it, and let us eat and be merry; for this my son was dead and is alive again; he was lost and is found" (Luke 15:22–24).

How many of us would have given up on the prodigal son? He was ungrateful and untrustworthy. He was unlovable. And yet his father said, "This is my son." How much more will our heavenly Father rejoice when we come in humility to him and rededicate ourselves to him in a spirit of service?

Can you match the prodigal son in wickedness? And can you expect any less from your heavenly Father than what he received from his earthly father? "For God so loved the world that He gave His only begotten Son, that whoever believes in Him should not perish but have everlasting life" (John 3:16).

The story of the prodigal son also answers the question of why God sometimes lets us fall so far. I often hear people say, "Why did God let things get so bad for me? Why has he allowed me to burn through my health? Why has he allowed my marriage to be destroyed? Why has he allowed my loved one to die? Why must I suffer like this?"

God allows those things so that when he is there to rescue you, to reset you, no one else gets the glory. Sometimes he has to use hard times to show you that it's not within your power to rescue yourself. The prodigal son's money, contacts, education, charm, all of it served only to help take him down.

People will disengage from you. They will give up on you. They will throw you away during tough times. That includes people who forget that they have been the recipients of the grace and mercy of God. But God is using this moment, this book, to tell you that he hasn't given up on you. God allows bad things to happen so you will know without a doubt that nobody but God can bring you out. God removes the things we are attached to so that we reach that point of surrender. And then, like the father in Jesus' story, he is waiting to lavish you with love when you call on him.

Jesus Is Called Savior for a Reason

Jesus knew the call was on him. He knew where his ministry was heading. He knew now was the time and he heard God's call as he prepared for what was ahead. He had spoken many times of what must happen, as he tried to get his followers to look at the world through eyes that had seen his kingdom. He asked them to think of things differently, to reassess and recalibrate their hopes and dreams for a new world where God was the only King.

Jesus knew that the long journeys, the preaching, the miracles, the adulation, the tender moments with friends and relatives, the faith of ordinary people, the strife, the rejection, the resistance from religious leaders, and the occasional pettiness, bickering, and incomprehension of his disciples would lead him to the cross. He knows our sin better than we do. He knew what it would take to save us—bring us back, reclaim, and rededicate us as God's children so we could fellowship with him.

Jesus spent time alone with the Father no matter what the pressures on him. He was in demand wherever he went. He was always accompanied by his tight-knit group of followers—relatives, friends, and disciples—and other times by a larger group of followers who would come to watch him preach, teach, and heal. And yet he also valued downtime. He would go into the mountains, setting aside time for prayer and meditation and for fasting. He knew his strength lay in his relationship with the Father, and those things nurtured that relationship.

In doing so, he showed us exactly where to draw our strength. We cannot be refilled and refreshed amid the distractions of a busy life. We cannot be nurtured if we fritter away time or energy. We need to spend structured time alone, building our resources, replenishing ourselves with the Word of God and with prayer.

Jesus knew the Word. He quoted Scripture often, drawing on it when preaching, when answering the challenges of his critics, and when praying himself. We are to draw, as He did, from the Bible's prescripts, its lessons, its stories, and its commands.

Jesus walked toward his destiny every day, reinventing the world through God's love everywhere he went. As he walked, he taught, he healed, and he reclaimed lost and broken souls. He *was* God in the flesh. No. Jesus *is* God in the flesh. That's the point of resurrection—a new start for us now. Jesus literally shows us who is calling us, who is beckoning us forward, who will lead us to our true destiny. If we stumble or fail or sink beneath what life has thrown at us, Jesus shows us who will carry us home. All we have to do is give him a chance. Step up and out of your ship. Accept a reset. Once we know what we are called to do, God's strength will support and supplement our own, and together we will stride steadfastly toward our mission.

The Example of Jesus

Finally, the time came for Jesus to enter Jerusalem. He knew what was at hand. You and I go into our missions and responsibilities not knowing ahead of time the hardships we will face. Jesus walked into his passion knowing full well the incredible toll it would take on him physically and mentally, but he kept walking.

It's worth noting again that Jesus was facing all this as fully human. Hebrews 4:15 says, "For we have not an high priest which cannot be touched with the feeling of our infirmities; but was in all points tempted like as we are, yet without sin" (KJV).

The pain he felt was like the pain we feel—the doubt, the strain, the anxiety were all there. By the time he prayed in Gethsemane he had reached the end of his strength as a human being. He wept. He agonized. It hurt.

But look at how Jesus handled it.

He shared his sorrow. He turned to Peter, James, and John, who were with him, and said, "My soul is exceedingly sorrowful, even to death. Stay here and watch with Me" (Matt. 26:38).

It is okay to share your sorrow, your doubt, and your anxiety with someone who might understand. It is perfectly in order to seek comfort from those on the journey with us. As we learn here, we may not always receive what we need—the disciples, after all, fell asleep—but Jesus shows us that we can look to others for support.

Then Jesus went a little farther off and fell on his face. He prayed, "O My Father, if it is possible, let this cup pass from Me; nevertheless, not as I will, but as You will" (v. 39). In fact, he prayed that prayer three times. There is no clearer indication than that moment in the garden that Jesus was

Jesus shows us that we can look to others for support.

fully human, and no clearer indication that he does not condemn us when we hesitate or doubt or become afraid of the sheer magnitude of what we are sometimes called to do. He understands our weakness, our desire at times for an easier road. But the key to all of this is in the statement, "Not as I will, but as You will." In that, Jesus tells us how we are finally to live. We are to submit to the will of God, no matter what the cost.

He went on to suffer crucifixion at the hands of the Romans, and as he cried out, "It is finished" (John 19:30), and "Father, into thy hands I commend my spirit" (Luke 23:46 KJV), we see the light go out. Never has such darkness descended on the earth. The great veil of the temple split. The earth quaked. The dead rose.

New Life and Good News

But if it had ended there, all would be lost.

"If Christ is not risen," says Paul in 1 Corinthians 15:17, 19, "your faith is futile. . . . If in this life only we have hope in Christ, we are of all men the most pitiable."

But Jesus rose on Easter morning. That is the Great Reset. The tomb is empty. Jesus, the suffering human being, is no longer there. Sin, suffering, and death will never have the final say.

Your old self dies in a reset. You are renewed. Your new self looks like the old you, and it may walk and talk like the old you, but it is new, able to do new things. You are reprogrammed.

At the beginning of this book, I used the example of my malfunctioning phone. When I walked out of the shop after getting it reset, its old nature stayed behind. It was gone. It is the same with those of us who are reset. The liar is not there. The thief is not there. The drug dealer is not there. The prostitute is not there.

Because Jesus rose again, you can rise again. Because he took on our humanity, you can take on his divinity. Because he underwent a human death, you can take part in everlasting life. Your reset can happen because you can tap in to the ultimate power source, the power of God that was shown most clearly on earth that long-ago Easter morning.

> Because [Jesus] took on our humanity, you can take on his divinity.

"All power is given unto me in heaven and in earth" (Matt. 28:18 KJV), Jesus said, and that power is available to us through his Spirit.

If Jesus is alive, you have no business being dead. If the tomb is empty, you can leave the past behind. Because he rose from the dead and lives now, you can rise from your sin, your distraction, and your complacency to live fully. You can bring new life to your job, your marriage, your schooling, your friendships, and your ministry.

To be reset in the power of the resurrection is to embrace

a new beginning. It is your chance to go forth with new life and good news. It is my chance as well.

Reset in Motion

If you think resurrection isn't possible, consider Steve's story. You may know someone like him. Steve was a Vietnam vet who struggled for years with Post-traumatic Stress Disorder, from the days before anyone had coined that term. He lived in a military town, and every time units were called up to face new combat, he found himself reliving the worst of what he'd seen and heard. Nothing stopped the memories that flooded back in. He tried church now and then, but gave up each time. He thought frequently of suicide.

Finally, one day he was sitting in his living room with a gun to his head, ready to pull the trigger. Somewhere deep inside, though, he felt God tugging at him. It was something he had felt before. He lowered the gun and prayed with a fervor he hadn't had in years. "All right," he began. "I'll give you one more chance." He emptied his heart and soul and vowed to find a way to be useful to others, even if he couldn't help himself.

Steve went back to church with his wife, but he knew he wanted more than just to attend services. He looked for something, anything that might need to be done. It just so happened that his church was preparing to send relief packages to soldiers in Afghanistan. He pushed past the memories and began participating. Soon he was heading up the effort. He began seeking out young soldiers returning from battle zones, offering them an empathetic ear. He wanted to give them the chance to talk about things they couldn't share with their families. He did it for them, but, just as important, he did it for himself.

As months turned to years, people noticed a difference in Steve. His whole attitude and demeanor had changed. One day, he stood up during a service and told his story. People who thought they knew him had no idea what he had been through and what it had taken to get him to the breakthrough he had experienced. They just knew he had gone from troubled man to beacon of light. He had become a living example of the power of reset.

Resurrection People

I have come that they may have life, and that they may have it more abundantly.

—JOHN 10:10

To be reset is to be on the other side of Easter morning, secure in your knowledge that Jesus is risen and you are one of his Resurrection People. It is the ultimate new beginning. Being reset reconnects you to the ultimate source of power and purpose. It allows you to regain your sense of mission and gives you the strength to carry it out. It is your chance to go forth with new life, spreading the good news in the way God has called you.

As his Resurrection People,

We are not downcast.
We are not apologetic.
We are not afraid.
We are resolute.
We are focused.
We are kind.
We are strong.
We have purpose.

Let's linger there on that word *purpose.* Everyone asks at some point, "Why am I here? What am I to do?" Your purpose was part of God's plan before the foundation of the world. "Before I formed you in the womb I knew you," he says in Jeremiah 1:5. Romans 8:30 speaks of us as predestined and says, "Whom He predestined, these He also called."

We were each born with a mission, a life purpose. We may lose track of it or struggle to find it, but it is there, and nothing big will come to fruition without that sense of purpose. Many of us recognize it as a passion. Not sure of yours? Ask yourself, "What dreams burn within me? What keeps me up at night?" If you separate the vain and earthly dreams from those truly of the Lord, you can begin to get on the right track.

Once you are clear on the passion, you are called to preparation, which is what ultimately puts you on the path. Plenty of people have zeal, but few have zeal tied to knowledge. It may take schooling, it may take inspirational reading, it may take practice and training. It will definitely take spiritual preparation. Being reset means you are working with God to do all those things. Done correctly, each of those things is a God-approved investment in you. Once you are prepared, you begin to fulfill your purpose, and a fulfilled purpose is living out your destiny.

To have meaning, to live out your destiny, it is important that your purpose is bigger than you. God, as we have seen, does not call us to easy. He calls us to hard. God is looking for us to bring our best to bear on his purposes, to reach beyond our grasp, to accomplish more than we would have thought possible. And now you have a step-by-step pathway.

You have great things in you! This is your time to shine. With God, all things are possible, and with reset, they are doable. Chase your godly dreams. Make them happen. God's kingdom needs you and your special gifts, and once you have prepared, God will open the door of opportunity.

Reset is about believing that God sees the best in me. And if he sees it and is aligned with me to make it happen, who am I not to believe? It's time to own the future, to declare that the rest of me will be the best of me. It's time to say, "I've got vision. I've got dreams. I will prepare. I will fulfill my destiny."

> You have great things in you! This is your time to shine.

As you sit reading this, there is a world-changing idea inside you. Perhaps it's a day-care center, a food business, a music ministry, a book, a nonprofit, a social or political movement meeting a pressing need. This is your call to go from idea to execution, from intention to implementation. This is your call to turn your dream into destiny.

Don't wait. This is the time. You have all the resources inside your head and heart to set this in motion. Connect with those who can offer information, insight, and encouragement, but don't look to someone else to do the work. God is saying, "It's up to you." Step out there, trust God, and say, "I've been reset for a reason."

When you are reset, you see more clearly. You hear more clearly. You think more clearly. Make your purpose something you live every day and know that God walks beside you, has scoped out the terrain in front of you, and will travel behind you, bringing up the rear guard and cleaning up your mess.

REFLECTIONS

- Do you follow Jesus' example of applying quiet time set aside for prayer, meditation, and Bible reading?
- Are you ready for physical as well as spiritual reset?
- Can you set aside your last, lingering doubt and commit to reset?
- Can you identify with the prodigal son? Can you identify as well with those who might have given up on him?
- Have you found your purpose? Have you embraced it?

ABOUT THE AUTHOR

Bishop Joseph Warren Walker III, DMin, is the senior pastor of Mount Zion Baptist Church, Nashville, Tennessee, with three locations, including virtual church at mtzionanywhere. org, and a membership of thirty thousand. The International Presiding Bishop of the Full Gospel Baptist Church Fellowship, he received a BA from Southern University, Baton Rouge, Louisiana; a MDiv from Vanderbilt University; and a DMin from Princeton Theological Seminary. Bishop Walker holds honorary doctorates from Meharry Medical College and Southern University. He is also a member of the Omega Psi Phi Fraternity and the Kappa Kappa Psi Band Fraternity.